D1615009

BRITISH VOICES

To my Father

British troops in Meelin, County Cork, during an official reprisal, 1921.

BRITISH VOICES

FROM THE IRISH WAR OF INDEPENDENCE 1918-1921

THE WORDS OF BRITISH SERVICEMEN WHO WERE THERE

William Sheehan

The Collins Press

Published in 2005 by
The Collins Press
West Link Park
Doughcloyne
Wilton
Cork

British Library Cataloguing in Publication Data

Sheehan, William
    British voices : from the Irish War of Independence
    1918 - 1921 ; the words of British servicemen who
    were there
    1. Ireland - History - War of Independence, 1919-
    1921 - Personal
    narratives, British
    I. Title
    941.5'0821

ISBN-10: 1903464897

Typesetting: The Collins Press

Font: Hoefler, 11 point

Cover design: Design Matters

Printed by Creative Print and Design, UK

CONTENTS

LIST OF ILLUSTRATIONS

British Voices

List of Illustrations

LIST OF ABBREVIATIONS AND ACRONYMS

Asst/Adjt:	Assistant Adjutant
Bde:	Brigade
Bn:	Battalion
Cpl:	Corporal
East Lancs:	East Lancashire Regiment
Sgt:	Sergeant
AC	Armoured Car
BEF	British Expeditionary Force
BM	Brigade Major
BRCS	British Red Cross Society
CDB	Congested Districts Board
CG St.	Coast Guard Station
CID	Criminal Intelligence Department
C/O or CO	Commanding Officer
CSM	Company Sergeant Major
DCM	Distinguished Conduct Medal
DFC	Distinguished Flying Cross
DI	District Inspector
ETA	Estimated Time of Arrival
FSR	Field Service Regulations
GHQ	General Headquarters
GOC	General Officer Commanding
GS	General Service

HQ	Headquarters
HM	His Majesty
HT	Heavy Transport
IDB	Illicit Diamond Buyer
IO	Intelligence Officer
IRA	Irish Republican Army
KOSB	King's Own Scottish Borderers
KSLI	King's Shropshire Light Infantry
LFS	Lancashire Fusiliers
LG	Lewis Gun
MBE	Member of the British Empire
MG	Machine Gun
MI	Military Intelligence
MT	Motor Transport
NCO	Non-Commissioned Officer
RA	Royal Artillery
RAF	Royal Airforce
RAMC	Royal Army Medical Corps
RE	Royal Engineers
RFC	Royal Flying Corps
RIC	Royal Irish Constabulary
RN	Royal Navy
RSM	Regimental Sergeant Major
SAA	Small Arms Ammunition
SPO	Stocker Petty Officer or Senior Petty Officer
WO	War Office
WRAF	Women's Royal Airforce
WT	Wireless Telegraph

PREFACE

Every effort has been made to reproduce the accounts in this book as faithfully as possible and to retain the original spelling and punctuation. However, to avoid confusion, in some cases, spelling errors have been corrected, and the presentation of the originals has been altered to meet to the requirements of publishing. Some readers familiar with the history of the War of Independence will note that the accounts given by some of the men contain errors of fact. A conscious decision was made to print these accounts without extensive footnoting or commentary on the text, so that the reader is free to read these accounts in a format as close as possible to the original documents.

Every effort was made to secure the copyright for each chapter in this book. While permission was given by the majority of copyright holders, regrettably, with the passage of time, it has not been possible to contact all the holders. The remaining accounts have been printed with the permission of the relevant archives.

I have attempted to provide the fullest biographies possible for each individual in this book, but in some cases, the specific details have proved difficult to trace.

WILLIAM SHEEHAN
August, 2005

INTRODUCTION

THE MILITARY CONFLICT in Ireland from 1919 to 1921 has been given many names: the War of Independence, the Anglo-Irish War or the Anglo-Irish conflict. All, however, describe a process that led to the separation from the Union and the creation of the Irish Free State and, ultimately, the Republic of Ireland.

After the 1918 election and the creation of Dáil Éireann in 1919, leaders like Eamonn de Valera and Michael Collins began a military resistance against British government in Ireland. This was to complement the political resistance and ensure the creation of a republic. However, the initial target of the IRA (Irish Republican Army) was not the British Army, but the Royal Irish Constabulary (RIC). During 1919 and early 1920, many police barracks were attacked and a number of policemen were killed, and the RIC slowly began to disintegrate. At first, the British government, under David Lloyd-George, responded by recruiting ex-servicemen into the RIC; these men became known as the Black and Tans. Contrary to Irish folk memory, they were not the dregs of British prisons, but ex-servicemen, many with distinguished war records; recent research has shown that many were Irish. These recruits, however, were not sufficient

1

to bolster a failing RIC, and a second group was created: the Auxiliary Division, RIC. Composed of ex-officers, this force was tasked with taking the fight to the IRA – something they readily did. They were also guilty of many attacks on civilians, and were largely held to be responsible for the burning of Cork in late 1920.

The British government – anxious to put further pressure on the republican movement so as to bring de Valera to the negotiating table – allowed the British Army to commence independent operations against the IRA in late 1920. Over the coming months and up to the Truce on 11 July 1921, the British Army placed the IRA under increasing pressure – a fact testified to by many IRA volunteers in their private papers. This pressure was shown to deadly effect at Clonmult, County Cork, where thirteen IRA volunteers died, and at Lackelly, County Tipperary, where seven IRA men were killed. This increased pressure influenced Michael Collins and Arthur Griffith when they negotiated and agreed to the Treaty with Lloyd-George and Churchill in London.

Those who are primarily interested in Irish history should also remember that from 1918 to 1922, Ireland was not the only campaign the British Army was engaged in, nor the only military threat facing Great Britain. The British were involved in the occupation of Iraq, a military intervention in the Russian Civil War, the suppression of a rebellion in Malabar in India, a war with Afghanistan, a potential war with Turkey, the occupation of Germany, and was contending with serious political unrest in Egypt. All of these placed severe demands on British military resources, and predisposed the British government to negotiate a settlement in Ireland.

More, perhaps, than any other area of Irish history, the War of Independence has generated a wealth of published material, from memoirs of those who fought in it to a multitude of works by academics and local historians, among them the accounts of Tom Barry, Ernie O'Malley, Dan Breen and C.S. Andrews, to name only a few.

But British-penned accounts have been scant. Many of the regimental histories ignore the War of Independence completely; for example, Alan Wykes' *The Royal Hampshire Regiment* makes no mention of the campaign, nor does John Downham's *The East Lancashire Regiment, 1855–1958*. Those that do – such as W.J.P Aggett's *The Bloody Eleventh: History of the Devonshire Regiment, Vol. III, 1915 to 1969*, and Colonel J.M. Cowper's *The King's Own: The Story of a Royal Regiment, Vol. III, 1914 to 1950* – give it only a few pages. Yet within the archives can be found a wealth of information on this subject.

There has been a considerable debate over the last few years over 'revisionist' history; indeed, a very vocal refutation of it by those who hold the 'traditional' view. However, as this work will suggest, all history must be continually reviewed, especially when new primary material becomes available. Nevertheless, this book is neither a work of revisionism nor review; it is, rather, an act of restoration. It seeks to restore to the narrative of the war the long-lost voices of British servicemen who fought in it, so that we can arrive at a more complete understanding of the campaign and the events. Some of the accounts in this volume may reinforce people in their traditional view of the British conduct of the war; others, I am sure, will probably challenge it.

Many of the accounts detail the tedium and boredom of British military life in Ireland during this period. They show the central role of sport as an important diversion for the troops in Ireland. Some of the stories describe dances, pubs and relationships with local women. The reader will also note that many of these accounts were collected or written in the 1970s, and that many of the accounts link the two campaigns: the First World War and the Irish War of Independence.

Almost all the stories deal with military operations carried out during the campaign, together with the issue of morale, and the army's relationship with the Royal Irish Constabulary and the local communities. It may surprise Irish readers to learn that many British soldiers felt that they were winning the war; indeed, many believe their victory was 'stolen' by the British politicians who agreed to the Truce and negotiated the Treaty. Many others are outspoken in their dislike of the war in Ireland and the nature of the campaign itself.

Commander De L'Faunce and Vice Admiral Baillie Grohman offer a rare insight into British naval operations conducted as part of the war, from the prevention of gun smuggling to the use of the navy in the re-supply of military and coastguard outposts, and the transportation of important personnel. Likewise, Flying Officer Penny provides a unique view of RAF (Royal Air Force) operations in Ireland during the war, from reconnaissance missions over the Wicklow Mountains to helping Alcock and Brown's transatlantic flight. The use of aeroplanes during the war is also touched on in the accounts of Field Marshal Montgomery and Lieutenant General Percival.

Brigadier Vinden provides an interesting view of life in the internment camp in the Curragh, including his friendship with Desmond Fitzgerald and a strange tale of a drinking session with Michael Collins. Captain Jeune, an intelligence officer, details the British experience of 'Bloody Sunday', the secret contacts between the British government and the IRA, and his role in breaking into Arthur Griffith's house. The use and abuse of intelligence is also commented on by Lieutenant Colonel Lindsay Young and Lieutenant General Percival.

Details concerning the conduct of raids and searches can be found in the stories of Brigadier Clarke, Private Swindlehurst and Major General Wimberley. The importance of the need for a political settlement is acknowledged by Field Marshal Montgomery, Major General Wimberley and Brigadier Vinden. Vivid accounts concerning the treatment of prisoners are provided by Swindlehurst, Lindsay Young and Vinden. The transcripts of Percival's lectures will be of interest to all students of warfare, not just those with an interest in the War of Independence. He gives a detailed account of his experiences in west Cork, particularly at Crossbarry, but he also deals with issues such as the use of artillery, tanks and aeroplanes in a guerrilla war. On a lighter side, there is the strange account by Wimberley of sending Gaelic-speaking Highlanders into a public house in Cobh to eavesdrop on the conversations of locals in the belief that, while most of the population spoke English, Sinn Féiners always spoke Irish to each other.

A reading of the above accounts will deepen the reader's understanding of the British side of the campaign. These stories offer a unique view of some well-known events and fresh insights into famous individuals involved in the conflict, from Lieutenant General Percival to Michael Collins. The only shame is that these accounts have remained in archives, unavailable in their entirety to the general reader for so long. My hope is that this book will restore some balance to the narrative of the war, and that it will provide a valuable resource to all students – both formal and informal – of the War of Independence.

A view of O'Connell Street during the War of Independence, looking from Parnell Square East, 1920.

CHAPTER ONE

Private J.P. Swindlehurst

Details

This chapter comes from a diary in the possession of the Imperial Museum in London, containing an account of Private J.P. Swindlehurst's service with the 2nd Battalion Lancashire Fusiliers in India from November 1919 to December 1920, and with the 1st Battalion Lancashire Fusiliers. While in India, he took part in the suppression of riots between Muslims and Hindus in Amritsar in October 1920. On his return to the United Kingdom, he was transferred to the 1st Battalion, and sent to Dublin. What follows is an account of his time there, including his views on Ireland, the IRA and military service in Dublin.

Diary
7 January
12 Noon

WE HAVE JUST been told the most welcome news, I don't think, we are entraining for Ireland at six o'clock tonight. You should see the faces, it's a wonder we don't step on them, they are so long. I don't know whether to post this on home or wait until I arrive in Dublin,

British troops barricade City Hall in Dublin, 1920.

there might be something of interest to record, especially if the Sinn Féiners start to be funny. We have a rumour going the rounds, that the favourite joke of the Irishmen, is get you to stand a bottle of Guinness, drink your health, and then crash you on the head with the empty bottle. We now know what the rifles and the other war-like equipment which have been issued, are for.

7.30pm Crewe

We entrained earlier than expected and at the moment we are stood in Crewe Station with all the doors locked, and an army of 'Red Caps' patrolling the platforms; but three lads have just done a dash and got clean away, good luck to them.

12.45am Midnight

Holyhead looks a desolate place at this time of the morning. We are just about to board two fast steamers bound for Dublin, after a flying train ride through the night. None of us had a chance to get out through the windows, we seem to have flashed through stations as if there was a war on and the enemy was winning. The wind blows chill, a blanket would come in useful just now.

3am

I have just extracted myself out of a heap of lads curled up round a ventilator to try and keep out the biting wind, and icy cold spray. This boat is doing a move and no mistake, I can just make out sparks flying out of the funnel of our other ship, it looks like a race, at the moment it is a dead heat. It's warmer walking about.

8 January, Dublin

We arrived at Arrans Quay on the Liffey at 9 this morning. All Dublin seemed to be out en fête to see us arrive, I bet they got a shock, we looked and felt terrible, cold, hungry and fed up to the

A group of British soldiers carrying out a routine search of a car in a Dublin street, 1920.

teeth. Stewed Bully and dried bread didn't improve our spirits, but the tea has been better. The CO of the 1st Bn. of the Lancashire Fusiliers gave us a welcome, told us what we had come for, and said we would all feel better when we had had a good sleep and a general clean up, he never said a truer word. We have come over here to finish our time, doing guards, curfew patrols, street patrols, and heaven knows what else. Ship Street Barracks, Great Dame Street is the new address, and it's raining, what a life.

The men stationed here regaled our ears with some lurid things that take place daily. The Black and Tans seem to do a lot of bloodthirsty deeds, but the Sinn Féiners don't seem far behind. I thought of chucking this, it might not be possible to get time to write any experiences, but I'll see later. On the backs down is the best place just now, Gilby at the moment has started to drive the pigs home so I'm going to do the same.

9 *January*

Gilby and I have just arrived back from the city. After we had cleaned up etc., passed the doctor, had a lecture at the same time, that the 'Colleens' are likely to put in our way and a hundred and one little formalities to go through, not forgetting the tin hat, to stop the empty bottles of 'Guinness', we were given a pass out until 9.30. The time is now 8.45, we thought it better to get back, after what happened to us. We were along Sackville Street admiring some 'civvy boots', when someone came up behind us and told us to 'stick your hands up' at the same time we both felt two hard things sticking into our backs. The voice spoke Irish alright, but we never saw a face, we were told look to the front and answer politely, and no harm would come. It seemed to be a long while before he finished questioning us, of all the questions, were we married? – where had we come from? – How long were we going to be here? – and I don't

British soldiers examine some captured weapons in Dublin. Note the Peerless armoured car in the background, 1921.

know what else. To say we were alarmed is putting it mildly, there seemed to be a general hold-up around us, all seemed to become very quiet. Our pockets were taffed from behind and after explaining what the contents were, the voice said 'Away wid yez Tommy down the road a bit, and you don't look back at all, now go', we didn't stop it would have been foolish to look back, so we made our way back to barracks. We have since heard, that a Sergeant out of the 1st Batt has been brought in shot in the stomach, he showed fight, silly chap, its no use when the odds are against you, I felt the situation keenly at the time, but what's the use. We must have given the Sinn Féin element something to think about, it appears quite a lot of us have been held up in different parts of the city. Dublin seems to be on our first acquaintance a rotten place to be in, people hurry along the streets, armoured cars dash up and down, bristling with machine guns. We have two extremely fast cars with Rolls Royce engines, we had a talk to the drivers this morning, and were told they are kept in readiness to catch the elusive Michael Collins when news of his whereabouts comes to hand. He must be famous, £500 is being offered dead or alive for his capture, but all the Black and Tans (who by the way seem to be all the out of work demobbed officers and men who can't settle down) and CID men from Scotland Yard, can't get hold of him. The men who style themselves as Black and Tans walk about like miniature arsenals, a brace of revolvers on each hip, bandoliers of ammunition slung around, and a short musket to finish off the ensemble. They dash about in cars with wire-netting covers at all hours of the day and night, bent on some raid, reprisal, or the capture of some Sinn Féiners. The wire-netting on the cars is to prevent bombs being thrown in amongst the occupant, an occurrence which seems to have been frequently done quite recently. The CO has a few words about being on active service, and being liable to be called out at any moment – what a coincidence, a sergeant has just been round and collared twenty

An IRA Volunteer fires a shot during the battle for the Custom House, 1921 (re-enactment).

men to hold up the centre of Dublin, along with a lot more, six lorries, with twenty men in each are just about to leave, Gilby has clicked. I have been detailed to mount guard at the City Hall for 48 hours at 12 noon tomorrow, so I must finish off for tonight, things are happening sooner than we expected.

12 January

The time is six in the evening, we have just had tea, the first guard is over. I feel a bit tired, it will be nice to undress and sleep right through till morning. How time drags, we do two hours on and four off, it feels the other way about, you hardly seem to have closed your eyes when it's time to go on again. It's a fine big building we have been in, but badly knocked about, bullet marks all over the place, rooms ransacked, mirrors and furniture smashed to bits. The central hall has a statue of Parnell taking up a prominent place in the centre, some of the attackers or defenders, I don't know which, appear to have bled rather profusely around it, the marble base and floor was badly bloodstained. The Sergeant in charge told us seven men were shot down near Parnell's statue, so things have been bad about ten days ago. The first night passed quietly, just a few distant shots to be heard, all the city goes still at curfew which is ten o'clock. Once we heard hurrying footsteps dodging the curfew lorries, but little else happened. Not so last night, opposite our place is the newspaper office of the *Dublin Times*. At about two o'clock when the presses were going full speed ahead with the morning news, two open cars drew up, and out jumped a dozen Sinn Féiners who began to shoot the place up. In about two minutes all the windows had gone, we overlooked them and could see the workmen hiding behind the machines, out of the way of flying bullets. The place is only five minutes from barracks, and the noise of the firing brought a party of Black and Tans on the scene, the result of the fight was two killed and three wounded, one Sinn Féiner

A section of British troops move through an Irish street in a combat formation, 1920.

deceased and two wounded, the rest were Black and Tans. We had them laid out in our place whilst the ambulances came and cleared them to mortuary and hospital respectively. The wounded Sinn Féiners came in for a lot of questioning from the CID, they were only young men, but typically Irish. The 'Virgin Mary' stood witness ten thousand times to the truthfulness of the answer, no amount of threats to shoot them brought any further news to what the CID men wanted, so they carted them off. I have since thought if we hadn't been there, that the Black and Tans would have done them in, they seemed very bitter, especially since one of their confederates lay stiffening on the floor. It does seem awful that there are men who will stoop to such dastardly actions as taking their own countrymen out of their beds at dead of night, and shoot them down out of hand, just because they have a different view to theirs, on how the country should be governed. The rest of the day until we were relieved passed peacefully enough, hundreds of sightseers came to look at the shattered windows. But the police took charge and kept the crowds moving, and life goes on as if nothing happened, although one can sense the undercurrent of alarm and anxiety in most of the faces of the passers-by. The constant shootings, hold-ups and raids are leaving their marks, one can tell by the earnest whispered conversations, the darting furtive glances, and the ever on the alert look, that many don't know what will happen next. We were on the main street when a lorry backfired, and instinctively people dodged into doorways, some stood still, but it just shows, that the greater part of the population are living in a reign of terror. If their sympathies are with the Sinn Féiners the moment may come when the Black and Tans appear and take them off for a grilling or worse. On the other hand their own countrymen may come and extract vengeance for a lack of sympathy to their cause. Even if they are strictly neutral and are content to let things alone, they may be shot down at any moment

A platoon of British infantry are preparing to leave Dublin in 1922.

by a stray bullet from rival factions whenever they meet. Taken on the whole Dublin is the last place on earth where I would like to live if I had a choice, but then I aren't Irish, that accounts for a lot.

13 January

Mail came to most of us from home, they all seem surprised at our coming here, well we are ourselves. Little has happened that we know of, it just seems to be a constant repetition of guards and other duties, we are more or less resigned to the situation. I have been detailed for guard in Jury's Hotel in Great Dame Street, our party, ten of us take over after dinner tomorrow. It is the headquarters of Dublin CID the lads say it is a hot place, we shall have to see. Gilby and I have had a pass out, but only for two hours, we had some chips for supper, but they were awful, done in olive oil or else wagon grease, I think it was the latter, we couldn't manage them.

16 January

The time is 5pm of the 16th, we on the Jury Guard have just had tea, incidents have been quiet and murderous in turn. The reception hall acted as guard room, a form and two chairs was all the furniture we had, the floor was our table and bed combined. I say bed, but it is my way of naming the condition of repose one can get on a marble tiled floor when we weren't on sentry duty. The days and nights have been a constant repetition of comings and goings. Secret Service men and detectives kept us on alert to admit them, the pass word on the first day was 'Gin' and altered every few hours to every drink that could be thought of. Prisoners were brought in occasionally, a few looked about all in, covered in blood, minus teeth, and numerous other injuries. After a grilling in one of the upper rooms, we could hear groans and curses coming down the stairway, a dull thump indicated someone had taken a count, they took them off to Mountjoy Prison on the outskirts. One of the

Field Marshal Lord French inspects a British battalion in Dublin Castle, 1921.

CID men took the Sergeant and I up in some of the rooms. This is the place where eleven out of thirteen officers were murdered in their beds on November 11 last year. In Dublin, time is now reckoned as since or before 'Bloody Sunday' which that day has been called. Most of the rooms were in the same state as left that morning, walls and carpets besplattered with blood, it must have been a ghastly business. Since then, the perpetrators have been hunted down. Three have been caught and are now in 'Mountjoy' along with a few hundred others, awaiting trail by 'Court Martial'. The nights have been full of alarms, shots, and bombs awakened the echoes, mostly after midnight. Early this morning I was on sentry at the main entrance behind the iron gate, when the noise of a motor and running footsteps caused my pal and I to look out for trouble. We got it, the runner was a secret service man being pursued by Sinn Féiners in the car.

They dropped him with a fusillade of shots, when he was about two yards from the doorway. His impetuous roll, knocked us into the hall, when were going to reply to them. In a few seconds they were gone, leaving a bomb in the roadway which failed to explode. The victim was luckily only slightly wounded, one through the leg and another through his hand. We don't know where he had been but a big party of men moved out armed to the teeth at dawn, so he must have got some information which was acted upon. It appears most of the Sinn Féin element hide out amongst the hills, and come into the city by various routes after dark, bent on some errand of murder, revenge or raid. They can get in easily enough, but it's the getting out that causes the trouble. Our men, Black and Tans, police and CID all hunt them down, when the deed has been done.

20 January
This account appears to be getting a little disjointed regarding the sequence of dates, but it can't be helped. On the night of the 16th

A smiling British solider and his horse prepare for evacuation from Dublin's North Wall, 1922.

when we were thinking of getting to bed, we were ordered out on 'Curfew Patrol' in a big army lorry. Five minutes after ten o'clock we set out to round up the stragglers who should have been indoors. We caught twenty men and women, mostly men without homes, women of the streets, one or two drunken cabbies, but none were armed. You should have heard the wonderful excuses, some were going to the doctor, one man had forgot to feed his hens, and was going along he said 'to see if they were asleep'. On the banks of the Liffey we chased a woman in and out streets, she screamed curses at us interposed with numerous kicks until we dumped her in the 'Bridewell' to go before the bench on the following morning. Some of the rowdy ones we sat on to keep quiet, our ancestors, ourselves and future generations were roundly cursed as only an Irishman can do. The 19th saw us on the streets patrolling the poorest quarters, whilst the CID searched the houses, nothing much happened, a few women spat at us, but that didn't hurt. A few prisoners was the result. A party of LFs got into trouble, the NCO in charge was taking a suspicious man away when the Sinn Féin came to the rescue, and in the subsequent exchange of shots, some children were killed playing in the streets. We are now called the 'Rubber Footed Murderers', owing to some of the dandies of the battalion wearing rubber soled walking outboots. It is a very regrettable occurrence, the City is blazened with posters, and leaflets describing the scene, I'm glad I wasn't on that party. By way of recompense the military authorities offered a military funeral but is has been refused. All pass outs have been cancelled to prevent the rougher element taking reprisals. The time is 9.30 on the 20th inst and we have just arrived back from a surprise hold-up of all civilians in Sackville Street. Fifty men in charge of an officer were ordered out in three motor lorries. I was in the one that went along the Liffey and arrived at the end of Sackville Street where a monument to Parnell stands. The other two lorries went up Great Dame Street arriving at the other end of the street at the same moment. The officer fired a shot, and yelled through a megaphone for everyone to stand still in the name of the King. We had the job of shepherding the unwilling ones along to be searched. The chap I was detailed off with was the comedian in the concert party in India, he was happy, answering the silly questions from nervous women. No one had anything to fear if they were not carrying arms or seditious literature.

During the excitement a man tried to get by us in his stocking feet. On being questioned as to where he was going, he replied 'Sure am be jabez I'll be just going to feed the old sow, no food has she had since this morning'. On looking into his bag, we found it full of army shirts and socks. My pal said 'Away wid yez now Paddy you'll be tilling that to the officer down the lane just now'. It took two jabs of the bayonet to make him see reason, that was the last we saw of him. I have heard since that he was one of the party of Sinn Féin who held up some soldiers a few days ago, stripped them to their underwear and sent them back to barracks in a tram, so he will wish he had never seen an army shirt before they have done with him. When we have little to do and duties are over for the day, some of us get near the main gates and watch the different parties come and go. There is an order out that all civilians must walk with their hands out of pockets. It's a bad day for the one who doesn't or forgets, he most likely will find himself looking down a machine gun from the patrols or an automatic of the CID. I felt a bit sorry for one old chap, they brought him in streaming blood, it appears one of the Black and Tans had been coming towards barracks and this chap was behind all the way, with his hands in his jacket pockets, so the Black and Tan turned suddenly and knocked him down and then dragged him in. He didn't seem capable of any dastardly action, but then we don't know, such terrible things are done in the name of liberty. People in England don't know anything of the conditions here, shooting occurs in different parts of the city so often that they become of no interest, unless you happen to be near the flying bullets. It will be a week before I write in this again I have just been warned for a seven days guard in Mountjoy Prison, what a heavenly prospect, I don't think.

28 January

Well! This date finds the Mountjoy Prison guard over. If I've reckoned the dates right it will be about six weeks before we have another trip. I think it is the longest week I've ever spent, the nights have been cold and wet, it hardly came daylight some days. We had too much sun a few months back, we could do with a little if only to cheer this miserable place up a bit. The inmates of the prison inside and their relations outside kept us lively at times. Every night a crowd collected outside the walls, trying to cheer up someone they knew inside, how some Irish hate us. I don't think anyone on earth can curse like a thoroughly infuriated Irishman. One night in particular, just after a large batch of prisoners had been brought in, the usual riff raff collected, and deluged the walls with rotten eggs, over ripe fruit and refuse out of all the dust bins in Dublin, the place smelled worse than some of the dirty Irishwomen do, until they are forcibly scrubbed by the policemen's wives. In one part of the prison Countess Markovitz a big Russian agitator had a cell, I had to watch her clean her cell up one morning. She said a lot in Russian about things in general, suppose I was included, but it didn't matter my Russian amounts to nil, so I didn't know a thing, her face was enough. The troops had most of the awkward refractory ones to deal with, the Royal Irish Constabulary didn't seem over anxious to deal with them. I think they had in mind what would happen to them if some of the lawless ones were able to carry out their threats of violence, and they were violent, nothing less than having you shot by Sinn Féiners. From the top of the prison walls, could be seen the hills which surrounded Dublin on three sides. To look at them one could hardly realise they hid some of the worst desperados and madly incensed men that ever lived in Ireland. They must be mad to do the horrible deeds. If this is for liberty and freedom what is taking place here now, well serfdom cannot be any worse. We heard whilst on guard that a party of Sinn Féiners ambushed a car containing Black and Tans threw a bomb in amongst them, and then shot them down one by one as they tried to get clear. As a reprisal the Black and Tans set out and cleared a whole street of inmates who were known to harbour Sinn Féin, any man who showed his displeasure at being turned out, was next in turn for a box. It will always be a mystery how many went under, incidents like that are not published. Could you credit the orders tonight, Gilby and I are down for the Main Gate Guard tomorrow night. The worst of the lot. All the big red tabs come through at the main gate, the Black and Tans have their grilling room, they are at it night and day, knocking information out of suspects and prisoners alike, and then carting them off to Mountjoy more dead than alive. What a hole to be in, it will be alright being stationed here when things are normal, but now! You are no sooner off one guard than you are down for another. Roll on the day of discharge.

31 January

Another guard over, it wasn't bad after all. I think it is just how you make it. The time during the nights passed quicker than in Mountjoy, there was always something going on, some of the Black and Tans had a word or two with us. It appears they are recruited by the Government to fight the Sinn Féiners with their own weapons, such as surprise raids, searches and hunting suspects out of their hideouts. The big hunt for the elusive Michael Collins take a lot of their time up. Most of them sport a row of medal ribbons, so that seems to be passport of entry into their ranks. To hear them talk one would think this trouble was made especially to amuse them and they alone. On the first night an actress coming out of the theatre a little way up Great Dame Street was shot in the company of a Black and Tan. We heard the shooting and saw the people running away, but didn't know until they dragged some of the slayers in, what it was all about. The rest of the night we spent listening to the groans and yells coming from the grilling room. The following day and night passed fairly quiet, some of the pals had a curfew patrol with a young officer, from their accounts since, they had the time of their lives. The officer in charge must have come straight from school, the 'ladies' they caught had really shocked him. A few days ago all of us who came from India were issued with a leather waistcoat as an aid for warmth. It has been very acceptable, especially when the second night comes round, and your sentry post happens to be in a draughty gateway. I think one feels the cold more when sleep is the one thing you would give anything to have. Here goes a few hours all in one piece, the time is 9.30, some of those on guard are already off. I'm about fed up with Dublin, the Irish and all their works, I suppose I shall feel better in the morning. A good sleep works wonders.

28 February

It is now a month since I did anything in this, that is bad work for a diarist, but only a few more pages will see the finish, so I must see it through to the end. I gave up, for simple reason, that each day was a repetition of the day previous, if we weren't on guard in some place, we were patrolling somewhere else, or else having a route march, and we seem to have had plenty of those. Night after night we have been ordered out, 'Michael Collins had been located, he was imprisoned in such and such a house, the CID had him surrounded', and all sorts of rumours. At the time of writing, he is still at large, and from what I can see of the situation he is likely to be, the population of Dublin are too loyal to give him away. I was going to say I hope he keeps free, but someone might see this before I get it home so that is better left unwritten. The ambushings, killings and raids still go on, how the people of Dublin stick it, I don't know. Only a few days ago, Gilby and I were going round by the Bank of Ireland on to Sackville Street, when a fight began. The place was alive with bullets, we dodged into a chemist's shop out of the way, and listened to the windows going. All was over in two minutes, then the ambulances were on the scene picking up the casualities. A young woman was hit, but not seriously, grazed her arm, she was badly frightened. She was someone well educated, her Irish was well spoken. Gilby and I got her to a tram, then we cleared off to barracks. We were out all over the place that night, bringing suspects out of their beds. Some we found in bed fully dressed, of course they came along. Others were in bed in their birthday suits, fancy that in the middle of winter. The only time we completely undress is when we go to have a steam bath, something like a Turkish Bath, but they did about a dozen at a time. We go in fairly white, I was going to write white, but we are a bit brown looking yet, and we come out like boiled lobsters. I did manage to click a cushy three days, when I was posted as court orderly at a court martial when three men were on trial for the murder of some of the officers at Jury's Hotel in 'Bloody Sunday'. They are now in Mountjoy Prison awaiting execution. I think I shall always remember their names and what they look like, they were called Johnston, Potter and Green, only youths, but the court found them guilty. Whether they are to be hung or shot I don't know, the presiding officer just said 'Guilty' and sentence will be pronounced in due course. I did without dinner one day to hear an Irish barrister pleading for one of the prisoners. It was a splendid appeal in all the pathos that Irish eloquence could command. If it had rested with me, they would have got off but the evidence against them was too overwhelming, the barrister spoke for three hours. My job was to escort the witnesses for the defence to the witness box. The trial being a court martial, everything was done in military style, scrupulously fair, anybody who could say anything in the prisoners favour said their little bits, but to no purpose, no other verdict could have been found. But I must forget that incident. There is a rumour going round that the Indian draft, that means us, are being sent to Portobella Barracks on the other side of the city, but how true that is I don't know. One thing that seems peculiar, is that we have had four medical examinations in the last fortnight, the reason I don't know, nor does anyone else. They must think we have brought some contagious disease from India with us. We have had some beastly weather, the barrack square has never been dry since the day we landed. One good thing all our boots have to be dubbined instead of polishing, we are a bit out of practise not having done anything in the cleaning line all the time we were out East. Which reminds me that I have never completed my notes I had on one or two things owing to our sudden departure from Lahore. So I think it will be the best thing I conclude with a summary and leave Dublin alone, I'm sick of the place, I think we all are.

CHAPTER TWO

Brigadier Frederick Clarke

Details

This account is taken from the private papers of Brigadier Frederick Clarke, which are housed in the Liddell Hart Centre for Military Archives in Kings College London. Clarke was born and educated in Leicestershire. He joined the Territorial Force in 1912 as a second lieutenant in the 10th London Regiment, and was promoted to captain in 1913. In the First World War, he served in Gallipoli, Egypt and Palestine. He saw service in India with the 57 (Wildes Rifles) Frontier Force and the 25th (County of London) Battalion (Cyclists) London Regiment. He transferred to the Essex Regiment as a lieutenant in 1916, and served with them in Ireland from 1919 to 1922. He was appointed captain in 1925, and attended Staff College from 1927 to 1929. He was a General Staff Officer at the Small Arms School in Wiltshire from 1930 to 1932 and served with the Essex Regiment during the Saar plebiscite. He was the commander of the Nigeria Regiment, Royal West African Frontier Force from 1938 to 1939. During the Second World War, he served in Europe and Africa, mainly in logistics and support services. He retired in 1947. Brigadier Clarke was the co-author of *The History of the West African Frontier Force*.

A motorised column of British Forces drives through an Irish town during the War of Independence, 1920.

The house at Clonmult, County Cork, after a fire fight in which fourteen IRA volunteers were killed in action against a combined British Army and RIC, 1921.

A LETTER FROM the War Office 23rd October, 1920 informed that I had been selected for a regular commission. On the 11th December I was gazetted to the Essex Regiment and posted to the 1st Battalion, the old 44th Foot. I was given leave for a month and ordered to report to the Battalion at Kinsale, which I discovered to be a small port on the south coast of County Cork.

The Battalion was quartered in ancient barracks designed for defence as well as accommodation, a characteristic of most, if not all, the barracks in Southern Ireland. The unit was, however, split up, and only Headquarters and one company with a few recruits were in these barracks. One company and the machine gun platoon were at Fort Charles about two miles away overlooking the harbour entrance. Then there was one company at Bandon, ten miles to the west and another at Clonakilty (to which name the locals added 'God help us') on the sea coast ten miles south of Bandon. There were also several detachments of one platoon.

I was posted to 'B' Company at Fort Charles and left at once to this old fort, which had been built during the reign of Elizabeth I. The mess and living rooms were quite comfortable, and the men's quarters were warm and dry.

The Company was commanded by one Thompson a keen fisher-man, better known as 'Trout' not only for his skilling this fish, but a facial resemblance to it. He had about 21 years service, had fought in the Boer War and finally commanded the 2nd Battalion in France during the autumn of 1917. He was full of anecdotes and strange names for things and people. For instance, doctors were 'farriers'; a clergyman a 'God-Botherer'; a perambuler was a 'spawn truck'.

I was soon settled down and got on well with the Trout who taught me a good deal about peacetime administration. As a result I was never in my regimental service called upon to pay for losses, which was the fate of a good many officers. A few days after I joined

British soldiers buy fruit from street sellers on Dublin docks during the evacuation of 1922.

'R.G.' turned up. He was posted to 'C' Company so I did not see much of him at first.

It was at Kinsale I first met Regimental-Sergeant-Major 'Bill' Bailey who was a 'proper Essex calf' from Coggeshall where the 'wise men' come from. When the Battalion was serving in the famous 29th Division Gallipoli he rose from Sergeant to RSM and won the DCM.

It was not long before I took part in a sweep to trap some notorious 'shinners'. Leaving the Fort at crack of dawn, with two sections of my platoon, we travelled a number of miles in RAF Crossley trucks to an arranged rendezvous with other parties and where we debussed. It appeared to me that this movement in trucks was unsatisfactory, not only did it give the game away, but one soon heard that the most successful ambushes of troops and police were when riding in vehicles. But, then, I had the value of a suspicious mind drummed into me at the Mountain Warfare School in India.

Having left the vehicles we moved to search a given lane with other parties on either side of us at a distance of several hundred yards. We saw nobody in the fields as we tramped over them. A sergeant who had been on a number of these parties told me, that the people were usually in bed until well after eight o'clock. We searched a so-called farm and found one old woman in bed sharing the one room with fowls, pigs and traces of a cow. The stink was awful.

The next was a better farm with two storeys. Having surrounded the place I went in with my sergeant and found the family at breakfast. I told them to sit down, put their hands on the table and keep still. I covered them with my revolver whilst the sergeant searched downstairs where he found nothing. He then went upstairs whilst a corporal searched the few outbuildings. Presently the sergeant rushed down stairs and was violently sick outside. I turned to leave and on going out a spinster with a nasty sneer, produced a bottle of whisky from a drawer and handed it towards me so as to show that my sergeant had forgotten to pick it up. I ignored the woman and spoke to the father of the flock, a decent looking old fellow, and told him I was sorry to have disturbed them. The sergeant would never tell me what horrid sight he had seen upstairs.

And, so we went on all the morning until about 2 p.m. we arrived at the final rendezvous with the other parties. Nothing had been accomplished by any of them which appears to have been the usual result.

The Battalion owned a large black dog of uncertain parentage. He was known as Niger and had been largely responsible for the death of two Shinners. They were up a tree, probably with the intention of acting as snipers. Niger passing with a patrol scented them and barked by the tree until the patrol noticed and shot the would-be snipers. He did not belong to any particular company but seemed to visit all in turn but not noticing any individual. He would always follow a body of troops he saw wearing equipment and leaving barracks, so he took part in many drives against the Shinners. He would go to Cork and wander through the barracks there but always found his way back to the Essex lorry in time. The locals used to say he was an emissary of Satan, and when he happened to be riding conspicuously, which he often did, on the leading lorry of a convoy, they would remark: 'There goes the bludy Essex wid the divil leading 'em'.

In March the Company was ordered to relieve the garrison at the lighthouse on the Old Head of Kinsale about eight miles to the south west of the town. I was detailed to go with my platoon. We lived in old coast guard cottages and suffered from intense boredom, bad rations, dust instead of coal and paraffin lamps. We were there a month and during that time were never visited by a senior officer.

To keep the troops amused I wired the area round our billet and constructed one or two fire positions. We had no means of contact with the outer world except by patrols. There was, however, a telephone to a switchboard in the local post office cum-public house about a mile down the track towards Kinsale. This was, of course, useless from the point of view of security. The following anecdote gives some idea of how we managed to ensure the secrecy of a particular little operation. One morning I was called to the telephone by an officer at Kinsale who spoke to me in kitchen Urdu:

'Salaam, Sahib.'

'Kya bat hai?' I replied. (What is the matter)

'Top ke chiz batti khana kewasti kai suba jehaz.'

This, of course, was not a proper sentence and his vocabulary was very small; but, after some thought and, repetition I translated it as follows: 'Artillery thing for lamp room tomorrow early in boat.' I thought about this cryptic for a long time then it suddenly struck me that 'artillery thing' could be some sort of banger for use by the lighthouse in fog, but I dare not ask the lighthouse people. The word boat seemed important.

At the crack of dawn next morning I managed to acquire a horse and cart. Then with two sections I marched down to the little landing stage near the post office. On arrival we saw a small steamer anchored close in Shore. Boats apparently loaded, put off at once and we lost no time in unloading the cargo which we found was consigned to the lighthouse and which we delivered safely. Needless to state that precautions against surprise were taken throughout the operation.

After my spell at the lighthouse I was loaned to 'D' company at Bandon, said to be a hot spot in more ways than one. Not only were the Shinners active in this area against the Crown forces but they had the habit of shooting their own countrymen in the back. There had been a big fire in the town about the same time as that at Cork – origin of both known unknown.

I went out with a drive with 'D' Company in which we covered many miles in trucks. But, it ended without any result. About this same time a statue of the *Maid of Erin* was pulled down during the night. This caused rather a panic amongst the superstitious inhabitants of the town. I happened to learn afterwards who did this. At the time it was put abroad that the 'foul deed' had been perpetrated by a column of 'Black Irish' from Ulster.

'D' Company soon went back to Kinsale and 'B' Company took over Bandon. They arrived with a subaltern new to me names Terence O'Cahir Doherty – this being his first visit to old Ireland. His father was the rector of Felsted in Essex where Terence went to school as a day boy. He was at once named 'Cyclops' by the 'Trout' as he had lost one eye on the Somme.

The following is an example of the treacherous tricks our opponents were capable of. We had no army doctor, but a local practitioner, ex. RAMC, looked after what few sick we had. He was not treated as a Shinner and appeared to be a well-educated man. One morning, after his usual daily visit, he asked me to come to dinner at his house and to bring the Trout. The superstitious mind came into play at once, as we had no social contact with any civilians of whatever political beliefs. So we declined. There is no doubt that by doing so we saved him from being mixed up in a kidnapping or murder in his house as had probably been planned by the enemy who had ordered him to get us there. I believe he was pleased when we politely declined his invitation.

We were very bored at being confined to barracks for so long except for small patrols round the streets of the town which did not serve any useful purpose. But, we soon had a little excitement, for the Shinners, quite contrary to their usual tactics, took the offensive against us and several other of the Regiments' detachments on the 13 or 15 of May.

At Bandon, it being Saturday afternoon the company was playing a football match with the police when fire was suddenly opened on both players and spectators from the edge of a nearby wood.

But not for long as we had a picquet concealed in some bushes who opened rapid fire with commendable speed and covered the retreat of the unarmed players and spectators back to barracks about 150 yards away. Unfortunately for us the picquet had one man killed who had only just joined after passing of the square. This infuriated the troops.

On the alarm sounding the troops were very quick at getting into their equipment and manning the defence posts, some still in their football kit. The Shinners, having failed in their first attack, opened fire on our barracks and those of the constabulary nearby. We located some of the attackers in the depression on the top of a small hill about 1,000 yards away and overlooking the barrack square on which a few bullets arrived. We also located some movement along the edge of a wood, which was dealt with by two Lewis guns, whilst I directed the fire of my platoon on the hill top. It was also discovered afterward that the company storeman, a veteran of South Africa and an old contemptible, had joined in by firing the stripping gun out of his storeroom window.

They soon gave up and I was ordered to take a patrol out. I chose the dead fellow's platoon who were anxious to catch some Shinners; and, it would have been bayonets if we had. They had managed to get away quickly with their casualties. The attacks on other detachments of the Regiment were utter failures; their morale was at a very low ebb.

About this time a recruiting poster all over the British Isles with an attractive picture of service in the middle east. It was worded: 'Join the Army and see the World.' One was soon discovered with the following addition: 'Join the Black and Tans and see the Next.'

At last plans were being made, co-ordinated from above, for sweeps to be made by columns on foot. It was, however, too late. The British politicians had arranged an armistice just when we could have quelled the rebellion.

After the armistice was signed we were no longer confined to barracks and were able to arrange bathing parties etc., for the troops. Arms were not to be shown on these occasions; nevertheless they were carried in the trucks, loaded.

A strange meeting took place at a chemist's shop in the town when a big middle aged man unknown to me said 'Good morning, Mr ——' I made an appropriate reply and he added: 'we could not have met like this a few weeks ago'. Then nodding to me he left the shop and the chemist said 'Do you know who that was?' I shook my head and he replied 'That was John Hales'. How did he know my name? Now John Hales, a big farmer, was said to have been descended from one of Cromwell's settlers, nevertheless, he had been the rebel leader over most of County Cork. He was murdered during the civil war after we had left the south.

The rank and file of our late opponents started to drive around in Ford cars and trucks. They looked rather a pallid, unwashed crowd who endeavoured to look important. As time went on they became bolder and stopped outside our barracks. One day they started to sing an absurd propaganda song of which the following is one verse:

Ireland's maidens, pure as snowdrops,
Shall I say it; God I must,
They were outraged of their virtue
By the hounds of England's Lust.

This was treated as a joke by the troops, and for many weeks, if not longer, they referred to the Irish girls as 'Snowdrops', and their comrades as ''ounds'.

One Saturday morning when the company was cleaning up barrack rooms a party in a large truck drew up and started to sing one of their war songs which commenced as follows:

40

We are the boys of Kilmichael,
Who laid the Black and Tans low.

Now Kilmichael was a particularly bad ambush and our troops
knew all about it as an army patrol arrived at the place very soon
after the ambush. They discovered the bodies of the Auxiliary
Police scattered about and abominably mutilated.

Suddenly every window facing the singers was filled by troops
who retoried with:

We are the boys of the Essex
So brave, so true and so bold,
We fight for the flag of old England,
And b----r the Green, White and Gold

Followed by some cocknies with:

Old yer rarw!
What did yer siay?
We kills all the Shinners what comes darn our wiy!

The opposition then departed.

The author of this masterpiece about the boys of Essex
remained anonymous. But, the song was sung again through the
town by a draft going to the 2nd Battalion abroad. This draft also
contained a comedian who swarmed up the rigging of the ship as
she was about to leave the quay at Cork, pulled out a Green, White
and Gold flag from a pocket, blew his nose on it, put it back in his
pocket, and came down the rigging to loud cheers. I think the
above anecdotes give a fair idea of the attitude of Thomas Atkins
after the armistice.

One Saturday morning shortly after this a gang of fishwives arrived and spread a lot of evil smelling fish on the pavement outside the barracks. Doherty, who happened to be orderly officer, was called by the commander of the guard on the gate. He went outside and ordered the 'ladies' to remove the offending fish. When I arrived a dreadful old fishwife was calling our Terrence 'a long legged gasoon'. He appealed to me and I told him to send for the Green Fellows (Royal Irish Constabulary) as, after all, we were supposed to be soldiers and not police. When the representatives of law and order arrived, the old hags departed at speed, leaving the stinking fish behind. Somebody had to move it, but not the soldiery. I suppose the Shinners thought this a good joke.

It must have been in the autumn of 1921 that we moved back to Fort Charles. By this time we knew we were going to evacuate Southern Ireland. How we hated the idea of giving this fine old fort, which had the arms of Queen Elizabeth I carved in stone on the front wall of the officer's quarters. We tried to get it out of the wall but found that it had been carved on a huge block of stone, which we were unable to move.

Every officer and other rank felt angry and ashamed as we marched out in the dark from the fort, which had been held by British troops for about 350 years. We did not see the rabble waiting somewhere nearby to take over the fort, which they never would have captured, but which our politicians had given to them.

The Battalion assembled at Kinsale and finally arrived at the hutted camp at Carrickfergus a few miles east of Belfast. We had observed a plethora of Union Jacks flying after the train crossed the border into Ulster and thought this seemed a welcome change after County Cork, but we were soon to be disappointed in more ways than one. It was not long before I found myself part of a two company detachment sharing an ancient lunatic asylum with a Highland Regiment.

The local Shinners seemed to be very careful about attacking the 'Bloody Essex'. But one day after being fired at in a street, presumably, we thought, by Shinners we captured a man with a hot rifle who turned out to be an Ulster Special Constable – so both sides were attacking us. Engaged in clearing a street one day an officer of my Company told a lout lounging with hands in pockets (hands in pockets being an offence) to take them out and move on. 'I will not move for an English bastard,' was the reply. The words were scarcely out his mouth before his jaw was broken by a rifle butt wielded by a sergeant behind the officer. This man was not a Shinner. We soon started to fire back without any delay whenever shot at.

A Sergeant Donnely with a patrol of eight men in the notorious Catholic Falls Road was confronted by a small mob who refused to move. He fixed bayonets and shouted: 'I was in a bayonet charge here in '08; there will be another if you don't move.' They soon did. The long shining bayonet of the Short Magazine Lee-Enfield always had a considerable moral effect when ever shown.

At one time we learnt that the Shinners were likely to throw bombs into crowds coming out of cinemas, etc., so we were ordered to disperse them as they had a habit of standing about before going home. One Saturday night I was confronted by a crowd who refused to disperse when I ordered them to do so. I spread my eight men across the road and gave the preliminary order 'Fix' very loudly. They began to shake out a little, but when I gave 'Bayonets' they scattered and we moved along an empty road.

About this time I passed the written and practical examinations for promotion to Captain. Walking about the slums of Belfast was hardly a good preparation.

In Carrickfergus, officers visiting guards and pickets by night were held up by dirty youths armed with government rifles. There was no excuse for this as on these duties all officers wore blue undress uniforms, carried a sword and were accompanied by an orderly NCO One officer who had the muzzle of a rifle pushed into chest by one of these 'constables' with his finger on the trigger. He paraded before the Commanding Officer next morning and complained of the constant disrespect paid to the King's uniform and danger to his officers. He announced he was prepared to resign rather than to submit to these insults by 'loyal' civilians. I believe that action was taken by our General.

As a matter of fact all ranks were becoming restive, too. The main cause was probably that we were being used as police, which is not the function of the soldier. Furthermore, it was absurd to see even majors trapesing the slummy streets of Belfast with eight men.

By now what little respect had ever been felt for our politicians had faded away. Added to which we were beginning to hear of the scandalous treatment of General Dyer by Cabinet Ministers whose dubious actions added fuel to the flames of distrust and dislike. The Dyer episode made a deep impression on the minds of officers who strongly felt that if they took any strong action, which was considered necessary to deal with circumstances arising in 'duties in aid to the civil power', they could not rely on the support of the Government. Some years afterwards when the feeling of distrust still rankled, the War Office was forced to issue a statement correcting this suspicion.

However, we were relieved in Belfast and 'B' Company and one other went to Ballykinlar, close to the Mountains of Mourne to fire our annual musketry course. The Royal Sussex, by whom we were accommodated, made a great fuss of us – they were old friends of the Regiment. A special guest night was arranged for our officers – before which we were warned not to stand up to the loyal toast. This battalion had served as marines for several years in the distant past. The Sergeants had a tremendous party and so did the other ranks. It was very nice after playing at policemen.

I heard there a pre-War musketry story of the time when proficiency pay had been introduced by the Secretary of State for War, Mr Haldane. 'An old soldier required a magpie (2 points) to qualify. He took careful aim, fired, and the butts signalled an inner (3 points). He stood up and in a loud voice exclaimed "Mr Aldane loses".'

A similar event took place on the last day of our classification when an ancient soldier only required one point for first class shot and his proficiency pay. He fired, and there was the ugly sound of a ricochet gradually fading away in the distance. He looked down the range as if to watch the flight of the bullet and then burst out: 'There goes my sixpence opping all the way to b----- y'

Our machine gun platoon had been exercising on the Mountains of Mourne and then joined us to fire their rifle course. Two privates were standing together cleaning their rifles when one of them pointed to the famous mountains and said:

'We ain't go no 'ills like that in Essex, buoy.'

'Bleeding good job tew.'

These pleasant interludes soon ended and we went back to Carrickfergus with its stinking foreshore on the Belfast Loch. The general excitement, however, had died down; probably the Shinners had gone to their civil war in the South, so we were able to do some badly needed training.

In September we left the 'Snowdrops' and moved to Borden in Hampshire, a few miles south of Farnham. We were all glad to be at home again in a good station. To use an Essex expression: 'I did not like myself in Ireland.' I do not think anybody else did either.

CHAPTER THREE

Brigadier F.H. Vinden

Details

This chapter is an extract from his memoirs held in the Imperial War Museum. He enlisted as a private in the 20th Battalion Royal Fusiliers, and saw action on the Western Front during World War one. He was commissioned as a second lieutenant into the 2nd Battalion Suffolk Regiment in 1916, and fought with them at the Battle of the Somme. Vinden served with the 2nd Battalion Suffolks in Ireland from 1920 to 1922, mainly at the Curragh Internment Camp. He was then in Gibraltar in 1926 and in Shanghai from 1927 to 1928. He attended Staff College from 1929 to 1930, and held an appointment at the Smalls Arms School in Wiltshire from 1930 to 1937. He served as a General Staff Officer, Grade 2, in Malaya Command, mainly in military intelligence duties, from 1937 to 1940. Vinden served at the same grade with the 1st Division in France in 1940. During the Second World War, he served mainly in the War Office, where he was responsible for improving officer selection and in the creation of the War Office Selection Boards. After the Second World War, he served as the Director of the Government of India Personnel Research Bureau. From 1951 to 1964, he also worked with UNESCO and the OECD.

Brigadier F.H. Vinden

Ireland 1920 to 1923

WE HAD JUST completed a year in Colchester, when orders came on Christmas Day 1920, to proceed on 1st January to Ireland. At that time, Ireland was part of the United Kingdom to which it had been joined in 1801. Demands for Home Rule for Ireland had been under periodical discussion since 1870 under Gladstone's Government and a Home Rule Act granting independence was on the statue book in 1914 when the First World War broke out. The matter was shelved, but dissidents in Ireland organised themselves into a sabotage force which murdered officers and soldiers in cold blood. One Sunday, around 7am, seven officers living in hotels in Dublin with their families were murdered in the presence of their wives and children. The rebels, known as Sinn Féin, had received smuggled arms from Germany during the war and at Easter 1916 had attempted to seize the city of Dublin. Fighting was fierce for some few days but the rising was defeated. Subsequently, rebel activity increased and when we arrived there were about two divisions of our troops in the country.

My regiment was divided on arrival, two companies going to Sligo HQ and two companies going to Boyle in County Roscommon. Boyle was a town of about 3,000 inhabitants with a barracks (as in many Irish towns) in which we were quartered. We were surprised with the mildness of the climate with the temperatures in January of 60 degrees Fahrenheit. There were some 30 or so shops, including a tobacconist who sold smuggled navy tobacco at a very cheap price. There was a weekly market, which began unpunctually, and there was no sign of open hostility, rather the reverse.

Our task was to assist the Royal Irish Constabulary and we had six lorries for troop transport. The help we gave to the police took the form of sweeps of an area chosen by the RIC and two companies would be lorried out to the select spot and circle an area of some square miles. On a signal all would gradually close in with police officers questioning all the inhabitants and making some arrests of able-bodied males about whom they probably had information. Some would be arrested and taken to one of the prisons. We also provided a guard for the country home of Field-Marshal Lord French nearby. He was then the Viceroy of Ireland. Our time there was void of excitement and we were confined to barracks except when on duty. We were not to stay there for long. The prisons had become over full and the government decided on internment without trial. Internment Camps had to be provided and we were sent to the Curragh to establish a camp to hold 2,000 internees. I thought that this was a happy choice, as our senior officers who had been 'inside' in Germany should know the ropes of guard duties and the wiles of prisoners trying to escape. On arrival, we found an extensive hutted camp established during the war and round it we had, with the help of the Royal Engineers, to surround the camp with two ten-feet wire fences with watch towers at each corner.

Aid to the civil power is one of the most unpleasant tasks which can fall to soldiers and our colonel, Arthur Peebles, was most alert to the pitfalls for the military. If anything went wrong, it would be blamed on the soldiers and officers as it is now in Ulster. Colonel Peebles wanted to avoid being in command of the regiment and at the same time be in charge of the internment camp. He induced GHQ to appoint a camp commandant for the internment camp, while the regiment only provided the guards required for it. He appointed me to be staff captain to the commandant and this brought me in a very welcome extra five shillings a day.

The internment camp was soon filled to capacity and amongst the internees were Desmond Fitzgerald, who became the Eire Minister for Foreign Affairs when Southern Ireland became independent, and Sean Lemass, who later became Prime Minister. I liked Fitzgerald and spent many an hour in evenings walking round the cage with him. He poured out the woes of Ireland going back to the days of Cromwell and the Battle of Boyne in 1690 when William III defeated the local chieftain. All I could do in response was to apologise for their action. However, we did talk of other things.

Colonel Peebles was correct in his forecast of troubles. The internees raised all sorts of trivial grievances and one subject which I recollect was a complaint about their parcels being opened and cakes cut. The reason was that the camp staff had found knives, files, letters and money in them. They dug a tunnel, which we did not detect and about 30 escaped one night. We foiled one effort in which an internee hid himself up to the neck in a swill cart and was found by the gate sentry who opened the cover. Other used to try and hide in the latrines or in the exercise cage, so that they would not be in their huts at nightfall and could attempt to cut a passage through the barbed wire fence. We were free of trouble for some time, but we later had a series of disappearances of one internee at a time. I gave much thought to discovering the method. One afternoon, I went down to the guard room at the main gate to see the officer on duty for an idle chat. I was looking out of the window of the guard room still half-thinking about the escapes and saw a working party of Royal Engineers marching out. There were about twenty soldiers under a sergeant. Working parties were almost permanently in the camp patching roofs of the huts which leaked or other maintenance jobs. I went out to the gate as the party was passing through and ordered the sergeant to march them into an empty hut on the opposite side of the road. I followed and was then at a loss to know why on earth I had given such an order. However, inspiration made me tell the sergeant to ground tools and when this was done, I said: 'I am going to search you.' This I did, making each man turn out all his pockets. From the pockets of the sergeant and four men I found letters from internees addressed locally telling the recipient to give the bearer five pounds for which he would bring into the cage a uniform in which the internee would dress and march out with a working party. They were tried by court martial and sentenced to five years imprisonment.

Thinking over our time on the Curragh, I have realised how frightfully 'green' we were. We never even thought of putting agents in the cage through whom we could have hoped to get some information. However, we did play one trick. On several occasions, the patrol which went round the inside of the cage after lights out had found an internee hiding in the exercise cage, either in a latrine or against a pole carrying an electric light, which had been rather sketchily encased in a sheet of corrugated iron. I took six of my brother officers into the cage one night about 10pm, we went into the exercise cage and after some minutes I fired my revolver into the ground and one of the officers then 'groaning' as if in agony. We immediately called stretcher bearers as in the trenches in France. These arrived – they were Suffolk soldiers – and an officer got onto the stretcher and we threw a blanket to cover him completely and he was carried out through the main gate of the camp. Of course, the internees heard the shots and were all looking out of the windows and the padre, also an internee, demanded his right to give last unction. The internees were quite convinced that one of their number had been killed or wounded. We had a list of the internees, but the hut leaders were supposed to keep lists of those sleeping in their huts. They were lax about keeping their lists up to date and as people sometimes moved from one hut to another, they were unable to discover who had been killed or wounded. We foxed them and had no more cases of hiding before lights out.

The 'disturbances' were far less disruptive of life than they have been during the current strife. In the 1920s the Sinn Féiners had no bombs and they did not have the support of Russia and Libya as they have today: and I have no recollection of fundraising in the USA. By 1922, the Royal Irish Constabulary and the Army obtained the upper hand, but the British Government under Lloyd-George became tired of the whole affair and decided to send for de Valera, the then leader of Sinn Féin. A call from GHQ while we were at dinner one night told me to release Desmond Fitzgerald and take him immediately by car to his house in Merrion Square in Dublin. As we had not been allowed to move without armed escort, I asked a brother officer to accompany me and we set off, each with loaded revolvers in our pockets. We arrived in Merrion Square about 10 pm to find a welcoming party gathered to greet Fitzgerald. Many of the Sinn Féin leaders were there, including Michael Collins, on whose head up to that moment there had been a price of £20,000. We were invited in and a good time was had by all. The agreement to divide Ireland was reached quickly and orders were issued for the release of all internees. As all money was taken off the internees when they arrived in camp and replaced by camp tokens, we had to return the money. Some internees were so anxious to get away that they went without their money and to trace some of them I got into touch with Fitzgerald in the effort to find addresses to which the money owed could be sent. In a series of meetings with him, he was very frank in expounding the difficulties of the takeover and also of the differences in the Sinn Féin Party. These difficulties came to a head in the civil war, which occurred soon after partition and in them, their hero, Michael Collins, was killed. One matter of interest which he asked me to put to Dublin Castle – the seat of the now disappearing British Government in Ireland – was a suggestion that Southern Ireland should take over the six Irish regiments of the British Army which were recruited in Ireland with drums and colours complete.

The Curragh Internment Camp closed, but, strangely enough, it was resuscitated by the government of Southern Ireland and used for internment in their civil war. A news item in the *Daily Telegraph* in 1973 announced that the Curragh internment camp was still in use.

Trouble then flared up in Ulster and we were sent to Belfast where we were billeted in the Usher Hall – officers on the orchestra platform and the other ranks in the auditorium. The centre of trouble was the Falls Road area as it is today, and besides bullets, there was a good deal of bottle throwing between the two religious groups. Our task was to patrol this area with a platoon at a time. We had no casualties, but assisted the Royal Ulster Constabulary, as that part of the Royal Irish Constabulary was termed, in searching houses for wanted persons. King George V opened the Northern Ireland Parliament, and hostile action ceased for a time. We were moved to Ballykinlar – a war-time hutted camp. I had received an anonymous letter while we were in Belfast headed by a skull and cross bones and with the words 'There is not room for you and me in this world and one of us is going to leave it'. Colonel Peebles decided it was best if I got out of the country and sent me on a three-months' course at the Machine Gun School, then located in Seaford, where I attempted to learn to play golf, less successfully, I regret to say, than I learned about machine guns. After the course finished, I returned to Ballykinlar where we were very isolated. In spite of our isolation we kept the troops interested, by lots of games and athletics and also by amateur theatricals. It was my first essay in this field and we produced Conan Doyles' *Speckled Band*. It went down well with the regiment and we then performed it in the Hippodrome in Belfast for the benefit of the British Legion.

CHAPTER 4

Commander B. De L'Faunce

Details

This is an extract from the personnel papers of Commander De L'Faunce held at the Imperial War Museum in London. He was a naval cadet at the Royal Naval College Osborne from 1912 to 1913. He served as midshipman in the HMS *Hercules* with the 1st Battle Squadron of the Grand Fleet in 1916, seeing action at Jutland. He served as a Sub Lieutenant on the aircraft carrier, HMS *Vindictive*, from 1918 to 1919, including a period of service in Baltic waters. From 1920 to 1922, L'Faunce sailed on the HMS *Badminton*, a minesweeper, which was engaged in coastal patrols off Ireland, mainly in supply and support role to coastguard stations, but also targeting possible gun smuggling. After his service in Ireland he served in both submarines and aircraft carriers in the inter-war years.

AFTER FINISHING THE subs courses I was appointed to the twin-screw minesweeper, *Badminton* and joined her at Southampton whence we sailed the next day for Queenstown. Piggy Morgan, the skipper, told me that I was the navigator and he expected our working relations to be the same as if *Badminton* was a battleship and I was the fully qualified 'N' specialist. Piggy was a navigator, and a very good one, himself, and this arrangement was excellent training for me, but I needed a lot of guidance at first in spite of my first class in the navigations course. It was a pity that we didn't have any long passages so that I could practice my book knowledge of astro-navigation.

The *Badminton* spent about half her time in Irish waters and half with the rest of the Mine-sweeping and Fishery Protection Flotilla at Portland. We were based at Galway some of the time, where we could take in coal and provisions, but spent a lot of time up and down the west coast with the object of hindering gun-runners – we never saw any – and in provisioning the isolated coastguard stations and their marine garrisons, and finally, in evacuating some of them, men and belongings and furniture too. This was not always easy. To load our whalers up with furniture alongside a very rough stone pier with a big sea coming in, and to tow them off to the ship with our dinghy and a temperamental early outboard motor, was a slow, laborious business.

We hit some nasty weather occasionally. We tried for some days to evacuate a coastguard station on our exposed bit of coast near Achill Head. Eventually the weather worsened and we got underway at dusk with the idea of going back to Galway, as we would soon need to go there to coal anyway. However, the south west gale set up such a sea that we decided to put into Elly Bay, an inlet in Blacksod Bay, instead. After anchoring, we set anchor watch as the wind was now storm force. I had been on the bridge since we sailed but stayed up until midnight, when the other sub, Gott, was due for the middle watch. The messenger who went down to call him could not find him. His bunk had not been slept in and a thorough search of the ship failed to trace him. We never knew what happened to him. Twin-screw minesweepers were generally very dry and it was unusual to take green-water on deck, but when we turned across the sea to alter course for Blacksod, a big sea could have crashed on board on the port side and swept him aft and overboard.

It was on leaving Blacksod and heading south for Galway that we had an unusual experience. I was relieving No.1 on the bridge as Achill Head came abeam some four miles off. It was still blowing hard from the west and a big swell was coming in from the south west. I was looking at the chart when Maclean said: 'Look at that – Port 30!' There appeared to be a depression in the sea a few cables ahead and to port. It did not look like a whirlpool, but the water was not breaking over quite a wide area. We only saw it as the ship rose on a swell and after a few minutes we could not see it any more and turned back to our proper course. The skipper, who we called, came up too late see it, and was sceptical – as everyone else has been who I have warned to look out for 'a 'hole in the sea' off Achill Head!

We were involved in one engagement with Sinn Féin. This was after the truce, when Irish were murdering Irish. We had occasionally delivered mail to a member of the new Senate who lived on the shore of the Kenmare River. We anchored off and sent in our dinghy with outboard, with an officer and one seaman. I was still on the bridge when the dinghy was on its way in. There was the sound of shots and I saw them splashing in the water round the dinghy, which Maclean quickly turned round and headed back. As the shots went on, I aimed the twin Lewis gun mounting on the bridge wing into the trees above the boat and let loose one burst. That stopped whoever was shooting.

We thought we might try to parley with our attackers and moved the ship opposite an evacuated coastguard station, which we had reason to believe was their headquarters. The men were at tea and the Captain, First Lieutenant, Chief Engineer and myself were having a cupper in the ward-room discussing what to do next. Suddenly there was a noise like hailstones on a corrugated iron roof. Our friends had opened up on us with a machine gun. I got up to the bridge, but we were out of effective Lewis gun range, and so I dropped over the front of the bridge to the forward gun platform where I found a stoker petty officer sheltering in the gun shield. The gun had been left with a shell in the breach. I finished loading, brought it to the ready, took gun-layer and directed the SPO who took trainer, and we put a shell through the front door of the Coastguard Station – a good shot. What effect it had apart from stopping whoever was shooting at us, we never heard. Our only casualty was the Chief who got a splinter off one of the guard rail stanchions in his trouser leg as he dived for the engine-room ladder from the ward-room. This drew blood but only just. We reported this 'battle' to Queenstown and were told not to try to deliver the senator's mail.

At Queenstown we were able to use the Royal Cork Yacht Club, which had a lively bar and served a good dinner reasonably cheaply. There was one of the old-fashioned scales outside the dining room, the sort like an armchair with a rocking arm on which one adjusted weights until it balanced. One day an elderly member was found mumbling as he rose from the scales after a good dinner: 'Most extraordinary phenomenon – most extraordinary phenomenon.' On enquiry he said that he had weighed 2 oz. less after his dinner than he had done before it.

At Portland, the seven sweepers of the flotilla, or those of them that were not off Ireland, lay alongside each other at the loading jetty, and went out of harbour frequently for sweeping exercises. There was great rivalry between the ships to put up the smartest performance passing sweep-wires and manoeuvring. *Badminton* was usually near the top of the league, and this may have led to her choice to accompany senior officer's ship *Sherborne* up to the west of Scotland for special trials. We made our main base at Oban but spent most of our time anchored at Kyle of Loch Alsh at night and doing trials with the new 'Oropera' sweep in Raasay Sound or Inner Sound inside Skye by day. It was a lovely late summer and early autumn and a very pleasant interlude.

CHAPTER 5

Flying Officer F.C. Penny

Details

The following details are taken from a memoir held in the Imperial War Museum in London. Penny transferred from the Australian Imperial Forces to the Royal Flying Corps in 1916. He served as a pilot and observer with the No.12 (Artillery Observation) Squadron in France in 1917, and with the No.36 (Night Flying) Squadron in England in 1918, and with the No.141 Squadron in Ireland in 1919. He was demoblished and returned to Australia after his service in Ireland.

NOW THAT THE War was over, we all wondered what the Air Board had in store for us in the immediate future, but having flown Bristol Fighters for many hours, I was posted to the famous 141 Bristol Fighter Squadron, then stationed at Biggin Hill in Kent. 141 was commanded by Major B.E. Baker, who had an outstanding record in a Fighter Unit in France. In the Second World War he became Air Marshal Sir Brian Baker. He was not a strong disciplinarian on the ground, but one who required every one of his pilots to be 100 per cent efficient in every phase of flying. He was affectionately known as B.E. Biggin Hill is reasonably near to London and opportunity was taken by most of us to visit the city at frequent intervals after our flying and other duties had been concluded for the day. After spending a few happy weeks at Biggin Hill, 141 was ordered to proceed to Ireland as a complete unit and I went with them. Administrative and other personnel proceeded to their new destination via Holyhead and thence by boat to Dublin. All pilots flew the Bristol Fighters first to Castle Bromwich near Birmingham, thence to Liverpool and from there across the Irish Channel to Tallaght aerodrome located about seven miles from Dublin.

When we arrived in Tallaght the aerodrome was occupied by an English regiment under the command of Major the Hon Oliver Twistleton Wykeham-Fiennes. This unit was occupying the Officers' Mess and all other quarters and our C/O Major Baker wished to occupy the whole aerodrome and quarters for his officers and men. (We were temporarily housed at various hotels in Dublin.) I well remember the acrimonious discussion which took place between the two majors. Our major won!

I was accommodated at the Shelbourne Hotel in St Stephen's Green. Although outwardly we were treated with great respect there was an underlying current of hostility against anything English, especially those who were in British uniforms. This was the time of the 'troubles', the Black and Tan, Sinn Féin era. Our aircraft meanwhile had been placed in hangars at Tallaght under strict guard day and night. After a few days in Dublin we took up our quarters at the airfield, established messes for officers, other ranks and WRAFs. We received warning that an attempt would be made to destroy our aircraft so we decided to place the aerodrome hangers and all living-quarters 'out of bounds' to all but squadron personnel. Guards were placed at strategic intervals with orders to fire if any intruder failed to halt. The first night this order was put

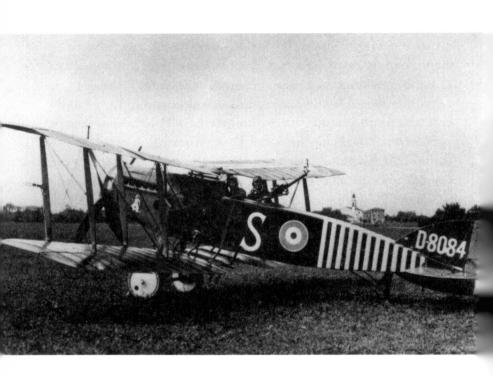

A Bristol fighter of the type used in Ireland by the Royal Air Force in Ireland during the War of Independence.

into operation another officer and myself were leaving the mess when we heard a shot being fired in the vicinity of the hangars. We rushed to the scene to find that one of our guards had fired a shot at a civilian who had failed to halt after being given the necessary warning. It was a simple story of misunderstanding. At one end of the aerodrome there was a quarry and the intruder was the night watchman who every night had been accustomed to walking across the airfield to take up his night duties. He carried a lantern and the guard, seeing the light, ordered the person carrying it to halt. The man took no notice, so a shot was fired, the lantern dropped and the poor innocent watchman ran across the airfield, breaking all records. He was caught, and my fellow officer and I interviewed a very frightened and subdued Irishman who was only doing what he was accustomed to do for many months past. We accepted his explanation and think he understood the reason for the order, which had been imposed.

Our presence in Ireland was for the purpose of keeping peace and good order in Dublin and surrounding areas. Information was received to the effect that numbers of Sinn Féin or IRA troops were undergoing military training in the Wicklow Mountains, which at their highest peak reached 4,000 feet. With our Bristol fighters we searched the mountain sides and glens but rarely found anything of significance to report. One important event happened about this time. Attempts were being made to cross the Atlantic from west to east with no success, until John Alcock and Arthur Whitten Brown, in a Vickers Vimy, made their successful attempt, but running short of fuel they were forced to land at Clifden on the west coast of Ireland. We had been advised previously of this attempt and were ready to assist if it became necessary. On being advised of the mishap the C/O with another officer and myself ordered one of our best transport vehicles to be made available so we could proceed at once to the scene. When we arrived we found that the Vimy had 'landed' in a bog area and had come to rest on its nose and wheels. Little damage had been done to the aircraft itself, so with the use of gear such as ropes, spades, shovels, etc., which we had brought along and with the very valuable assistance of dozens of Irish villagers, we were able to get the machine on to an even keel and by towing, pulling and shoving we moved it to a position where in the opinion of Capt Alcock he could take off. Only sufficient petrol was put in the tanks for the flight to England where they arrived safely. They received a wonderful welcome on the completion of this most meritorious flight, the first west to east flight from the United States. They received a well-deserved knighthood and I think a prize of £10,000. We were very happy to have been of some assistance to these very brave airmen whose flight was a momentous event in aviation history.

On a number of occasions we had as our guests to dinner in the mess a few of the senior Black and Tan officers, one of whom lived with his wife in a small cottage near the aerodrome. This particular officer returned to the cottage about midnight one night after dining with us, and at 1.00 a.m. there was a knock at his door and when he opened it he was shot with a revolver and died almost immediately. His wife reported the incident to us but did not know the identity of her husband's assailant. Such was the intense dislike of the Black and Tans by the Sinn Féin movement. We were all greatly shocked by this incident.

Following on this, our CO decided to stage a demonstration in the village square at Tallaght, which had a population of approximately 500. We had an excellent brass band and about fifty of us, all officers, marched to the accompaniment of patriotic airs along the half mile of road leading to the centre of the village, where we formed up in a circle with the band in the centre. The band began such well known tunes as 'Rule Britannia', 'There'll always be an England' and similar songs for about half an hour. Naturally a large

crowd gathered, not looking terribly happy though. We rounded of
the little demonstration with the band playing the National
Anthem, during which, of course, all officers stood at the salute.
Civilians usually taking off their hats for same, not so the villagers.
To put it mildly, this greatly displeased our CO. One has to remember at this juncture that we were all under quite an emotional strain
because of the murder of a loyal man who was doing his duty. Those
who had not removed their hats soon had them removed by the
CO who pulled them off and stood on them. This action was naturally resented, by the 'locals'. We then formed up and marched
back to our quarters. This incident brought a severe reprimand
from headquaters, and rightly so, I suppose, but there had been
some provocation.

   In Dublin itself many minor incidents were taking place, culminating in an organised march of some 20-30,000 rebellious
Irishmen, who had assembled in Phoenix Park before marching
along one side of the Park to O'Connell Street, which is the main
street, over the Liffey River. When they reached the Post Office,
which had been completely destroyed in the 1916 rebellion and was
in the process of being re-built, they tore down the scaffolding
breaking it into small pieces, thus arming themselves with a
weapon, which could be easily carried and used. Stones and iron
bars were also carried, in fact anything they could lay their hands
on which could be used as a weapon. We had been advised of this
intended march and were asked to assist the Dublin Metropolitan
Police. We were each issued with a revolver with orders to use them
only if our lives or those of the police were endangered. We arrived
at the O'Connell Bridge to find a solid line of police standing shoulder to shoulder across the Bridge. They were armed with batons
only. I reported to the police officer in charge, who appreciated the
assistance offered, but he asked us not to take part unless it was
absolutely necessary. The Dublin Metropolitan Police were an

imposing body of men, none under six feet high. They waited there in line whilst the rebels came forward in a solid body, shouting most uncomplimentary remarks against the police, who, though Irishmen themselves were daring to oppose them in order to preserve some peace and order. The officers in charge remained perfectly still, until sticks and stones began to fly, when the pre-arranged signal of one blast of the 'chief's' whistle was given and one command 'forward'. The police moved forward in the solid line using their batons with great effect. I do not remember ever seeing before or since a more disciplined movement than this one. So effective was it that in a matter of minutes the on-coming crowd turned and ran, leaving their weapons strewn along the street. I know that many Irish families we got to know very well deplored this kind of demonstration as it did the cause no good whatsoever and only tended to intensify the feeling that existed between those who felt that the presence of the English in Southern Ireland was justified, and those who would go to any lengths to get rid of them.

Frequently we gave demonstrations of close formation flying, usually over Dublin itself, sometimes with one flight and occasionally with the whole squadron. Our CO, who was such an excellent pilot, with two or more experienced pilots, often took off in tight formation with wing tips overlapping and flew very low over the streets of the city.

I think it was Empire Day or the King's birthday that we decided to use the whole squadron for a close formation flight in a 'special' display. I had not done very much close formation flying or not as close as our CO desired. We took off from Tallaght with the CO's flight leading, and kept in this close order as we flew over the city, finally turning to fly at almost roof top level, up O'Connell Street over the Liffey. Just what these displays were intended to prove, I know not, but we enjoyed flying our Bristol Fighters and we had a lot of fun. On one occasion I had to fly to Curragh an old established army camp, situated about 40 miles west of Dublin. Apparently the troops' pay had gone astray and some arrangements were made with a bank in Dublin to transfer money to the Curragh bank, and because of the time factor, this had to be taken by air. With my observer Lieut. Harry Boniface (Bonny), we took off in rather adverse weather conditions, but landed safely at Curragh, handed over the money to the Army Adjutant and took off for our return flight. A fairly strong north wind had risen and dense fog covered the route back to Tallaght. Both Bonny and I had received invitations to play tennis in the afternoon with some of our Irish friends and naturally we were anxious to get back as soon as possible. We could see neither the sky nor the ground and had to proceed entirely by compass. I had no accurate means of determining my 'drift' which I felt was taking me too far southward. After flying for some time and not knowing my exact position I turned due north and a few minutes later found myself in this thick fog facing one of the highest peaks in the Wicklow mountains. Knowing that the maximum height was not above 4,000 feet I made a sharp turn full throttle and quickly ascended to 4,500 feet, only to find that as far as I could see north, south, east or west, there was a complete ground cover of heavy fog. We were in the bright sunshine above but not even a small gap appeared which would enable us to see the ground below. I continued to fly north, both Bonny and I closely watching for a break in the cloud cover. After flying for about twenty minutes we saw immediately below us the centre circle of our aerodrome at Tallaght. With full throttle I dived through this gap in the clouds closely watching my altimetre for I had no means of knowing how high the clouds were above the ground level of our airfield.

On breaking through I found that I had about 300 feet clearance which was sufficient for me to locate my position and ultimately make a safe landing – very thankful to be on *Terra Firma*. Bonny and I, although a little late, were able to keep our tennis appointment. By today's standard, with up-to-date sophisticated instruments, this would not have been regarded as a hazardous flight, but all we had was an altimetre, compass, rev-counter and speedometre, no turn and bank indicator or other helpful instruments, such as those in modern aircraft. This incident firmed the close friendship that I had with Bonny and we had many happy times together in our off duty hours.

After the War he elected to stay in the RAF, became a pilot and spent some years in India. In the Second World War he was Adjutant at Hucknall, Notts. and figured prominently in the book, *The One That Got Away* by Kendall Burt and James Lessor, which related to a German pilot Franz von Werra, forced down in Notts, who eventually escaped to the USA and then Canada. My wife and I (especially my wife!) carried out regular correspondence with Bonny and his wife Ann, who later lived at Over Wallop in Hants. In later years when on a visit to England in 1947 and again with my wife in 1952, we spent many happy hours talking of our shared experiences in 141 squadron in Ireland.

Another firm friendship formed amongst the officers of 141 squadron was with Wireless Officer Lieut. F.S. Mockford (Stan), an outstanding authority on radio. He began his long and varied career in wireless and radio in 1915 whilst serving in the RFC and afterwards as an Air Ministry Official from 1919-1930. He made a great contribution in wireless and radio in Civil Aviation and was first examiner of candidates for an Air Operator's Licence. He devised the first phonetic alphabet and introduced the distress call MAYDAY. In 1930 he joined the Marconi Company and in 1935 became Manager of the company's aircraft department. He was also interested in the possibilities of radio as a means of air to ground communication and vice-versa, and was responsible for the technique and introduction of this system to civil Aviation and the RAF. Those who fly today realise the value of this method of communication without which flying would be a far more hazardous occupation. Our friendship with the Mockford family who lived at Chelmsford, Essex, was a lasting one and on our various visits to England we enjoyed their hospitality, myself on a business trip in 1947, my wife in 1949, and together in 1952 and 1960. Stan and his wife Win intended visiting us in Australia in 1961 when he retired and when we said our 'goodbyes' at Tilbury where they had driven us and had lunch with us on the ship, little we thought that we would not meet again. A serious illness overtook Stan and after surgery he died the following year in April. Many other friendships were made amongst the officers of 141 squadron, but these two, Bonny and Stan, were the best.

A large unit such as ours, consisting of pilots, administrative officers, WRAFS and aircraftsmen, now more or less on a peace-time basis needed some form of organised activities to sustain their interest. The pilots were not in this category, as we had our Bristol Fighters and an unlimited supply of gasoline. This enabled us to visit various parts of Ireland without any transport difficulties. For those who were interested in sport we arranged a special sports meeting, tennis tournaments and special flights for our WRAF (Womens' Royal Air Force) staff. With very few exceptions all WRAF staff took advantage of this offer of a 'sightseeing flight' and considered it a real highlight.

I was asked to arrange all details for a sports meeting and this proved very successful for we had many good athletes amongst members of the squadron. Special events were included for the WRAF staff who entered these competitions with much enthusiasm. Having had some success in high jumping I entered myself for this event and had little difficulty in winning it at (I think) 5 feet 7 inches. The enthusiasm and interest shown by our CO, Major Baker, in this sports meeting and indeed all phases of athletics helped considerably to make this meeting an unqualified success.

In so far as I was personally concerned, he suggested that I should enter for the high jump event in a combined RAF (all Ireland) sports meeting in Dublin. This I did and was again successful. Two other important meetings were in the offing. One combined RAF squadrons to be held at Stamford Bridge, London, and two inter-services championships later at the same venue, both of which I was urged by our CO to nominate for. In the meantime, however, an official communication was received from the Australian authorities in London, requesting that I should place myself at their disposal for repatriation back to Australia. This did not please the CO as he wished me to remain with 141 squadron at least until the two forthcoming athletic meetings were over. The honour of an athletic win for 141 squadron was important to him. So he, in his forthright manner, wrote to the Australian authorities stating in no uncertain terms that Flight Lieut. F.C. Penny was doing important work with the squadron and was therefore indispensable! This explanation was apparently accepted, at least for the time being, and so I was nominated for the high jump events. In the meantime arrangements were in hand to hold an aerial derby open to RAF squadrons from Collinstown, Baldonnell, Oranmore, and of course our own squadron at Tallaght, which was to be the starting and finishing point for the race. Bonny and I worked on our own Bristol Fighter and my aircraftsman reduced the wing incidence and retuned the engine, which enabled me to reach a top speed of 127 mph. The event attracted a large number of entries and included various types of aircraft. Our own squadron at Tallaght contributed eight entries, all Bristol Fighters. With Bonny as my navigator, we were flagged off from the starting point in the early afternoon and made good progress to the first check point. The engine was performing well and the navigation accurate. On the second leg we passed several other competitors and on checking our watches and maps considered that we had a good chance of winning this event, if our speed and accuracy could be maintained.

We reached our final turning point on good time and proceeded on our direct course back to Tallaght. The Bristol Fighter had two gasoline tanks, one gravity fed and located in the centre section of the upper wing, and the other on which the pilot sat, using a hand pressure pump to force the fuel to the gravity tank above. Noticing that the gravity tank gauge showed 'low' I started to pump in order to transfer gasoline from the pressure tank to gravity tank, but with no effect. By this time the gauge was showing 'empty' and I began to search for a suitable place to make a 'forced landing'. I had one small field in view, the surface of which seemed reasonable, but it was the smallest on which I had ever attempted to land a Bristol Fighter. Flying at only 500 feet I had no option but to attempt a landing and using an almost vertical side slip decreased my forward speed which was sufficient to allow me to get over the nearest hedge. I used all the well-known methods of reducing forward speed such as 'swish-tailing', finally landing at the lowest possible speed with my propeller (which was now stopped) pushing itself into a box-thorn hedge. Fortunately no damage was done but I had no means of rectifying the trouble, so leaving Bonny in charge I walked to the nearest road and persuaded an Irish farmer to lend me his bicycle so that I could get to a telephone to call for mechanical help from the nearest RAF station, which happened to be Oranmore. Although the Irish farmer had mentioned telephone I found that there was only a small country post office with no telephone so I had to send a telegram. In due course a lorry with mechanics arrived and rectified the trouble, which was a blocked feed pipe. By this time it was getting late and I still had to get out of this small field and knowing the distance I still had to fly to reach Tallaght I knew that it would be dark before reaching the squadron. I requested the Oranmore staff to telephone Tallaght giving our approximate ETA and asked for flares to be laid out. The Bristol

Fighter was a very stable aircraft with few or no vices. Its landing speed, however, was about 80 mph and at night time with limited lighting facilities, it was not always an easy machine to land. We landed safely, glad to be back, especially as a heavy fog was beginning to drift across the aerodrome, which would have made more difficulties for landing. While I was away competing in this little aerial derby, word had been received from the RAF athletic sports committee in London requesting me to report at Stamford Athletic Ground, London west. It would have taken too long to have reached London by boat and train, so I used my Bristol Fighter, flying up to Larne in the North and crossing over to Stranraer in Scotland. This was the shortest water crossing. I landed at an airfield just outside London where I was accommodated by the unit stationed there. Next day I reported to Stamford Bridge where I was given a programme of events and a number 6! I went to the dressing room to change and then had a run around the course to loosen up, then had a few jumps over the stick and that was all until next day, the day of the event. There were, if I remember rightly, twelve competitors for this event, amongst them an RAF Sgt Major who had won this event on four previous occasions. There was considerable betting on this event. Unfortunately I did not have anything on myself and the Sgt Major was 'odds on' favourite to win. We started the jumps about 2.00 p.m. and by the time the horizontal bar had been raised to 5 feet 8 inches quite a number of the competitors had fallen out, in fact, now I remember only the Sgt/Major and myself were left in the competition when 5 feet 9 was reached. By today's standards this height is not high, but it must be remembered that we were all amateurs and had not had any previous experience, or training. If I remember rightly again, the Sgt/Major and I tied for this even at 5 feet 9 and a half inches. I was quite happy with the result, having tied with the reigning champion of the RAF. As the reward was a gold medal for first and a silver one for second place, we tossed – and I lost, and the medals had to be returned to the maker, first to tie, and second to tie. I knew that my CO would be happy to know the result so I sent him a telegram. After spending a few days in London I returned to Tallaght where I received congratulations all around, another honour for 141!

Life went on as usual in the squadron until a date was set for the Inter-Services Championship, to be held at Stamford Bridge. I stuck a stick up somewhere on the aerodrome and when I felt like it, I took a jump! This was all the preparation I had for the big event. A few days before the event I travelled down again by Bristol Fighter near London, I think it was Uxbridge. Arrangements had been made for me to take advantage of a trainer who had previously trained competitors for the Olympic Games. I'm afraid I did not spend a lot of time with him. London was only a bus ride away and always held a great attraction for me, as it did indeed for a great number of the Australians. The afternoon before the big event I did spend a few hours with the trainer loosening up my muscles by vigorous massage and heat treatment after which he suggested that I take a gentle run around the track, which I did but on the way back to the dressing room I noticed some of the competitors having a little practice over the horizontal bar. I joined them, but wearing my sand shoes and the grass being damp my right foot slipped and I strained my ankle, not seriously, but enough to cause me to limp back to my trainer, whose comments could not very well be repeated here! He had given me strict instructions that I was not to jump over the bar and I had disobeyed him. I know he had good reason to be annoyed. Apparently he still thought there was a possibility of my winning this event so he spent a lot of time with heat lamps, finally binding the strained ligaments with an elastic bandage. He sent me back to my quarters to rest. At noon the following day he gave me further treatment after which I felt I could give a reasonably good account of myself in the event.

There were three entries from each of the three services, Army, Navy and Airforce. The horizontal bar was set up first at 5 feet 6 inches, which height presented no problems to any of us. It was then raised one inch after each successful clearance. We all cleared 5 feet 8 inches, but at 5 feet 8 and half inches the Navy team failed and so were out of the running. The Army team continued to 5 feet 9 inches but failed to reach the next half inch as did one of the RAF competitors. The Sgt Major with whom I had tied previously and I remained in the contest. Neither of us had before reached this height, and the bar seemed awfully high to me. It was not yet over. The bar was still being raised, half inch after each successful jump. We both succeeded clearing the bar at 5 feet 11 inches. The next half inch proved the crucial height for both of us. I missed my first jump as he did, but I was successful at the second attempt. Unfortunately for him he missed with his next two tries, which gave me the championship at 5 feet 11 and half inches. I was naturally elated, not for myself only but also for the RAF AND my own squadron 141. I sent a telegram to the CO Major Baker. I wonder if Air Marshal Sir Brian Baker would still remember the young Australian who won these athletic events? In due course I received from the RAF committee through Goldsmiths and Silversmiths Co Ltd, of London, a 22 carat gold medallion to commemorate the event. On the obverse side, the three services are depicted, Navy a warship, Army a tank and Airforce an aeroplane in flight. The other side bore the inscription 'Presented to Lieut. F.C. Penny'. This, of course, is one of my treasured possessions.

I returned to Dublin a few days later to find that another letter had been received from the Australian authorities in London, requesting me to report for repatriation back to Australia and as my CO had no valid reason for retaining my services, I made arrangements to go to London. I handed over my administrative duties, attended three farewell parties, Officers' Mess, Mess and

WRAF and said a very regretful farewell to all my good friends in 141, and this time took the boat from North Wall, Dublin to Holyhead and from there by train to London, where I reported to the Australian Headquarters. They posted me to a repatriation camp at Flowerdown near Winchester.

When I arrived here I discovered that I had met the CO previously. He suggested that if I were not in a hurry to return to Australia he would be happy to have me on his staff as one of his officers, a job which involved taking charge of groups of officers who were being repatriated back to the countries from whence they had come. Frequent visits were made to Tilbury Southampton, Plymouth and Liverpool. On occasions there were as many as 30-40 officers, many of them senior to me, and when their ship sailed from Liverpool it was necessary to arrange overnight accommodation in London. It would need no stretch of imagination to understand their desire to have what to them was 'a somewhat riotous time', on their last night in London. There was little I could do about it, but to put them on their honour to report to me at a given London station the following morning.

A passage was arranged for me on the *Indarra* sailing early December, but just before sailing time I was asked to give my cabin to a woman who, because of emergency, wanted to leave England immediately. This I agreed to do and ultimately sailed on the *Orsova* in the same month. We were in Gibraltar on Christmas Day and after a most happy voyage, returned home to Australia in January 1920 after a most eventful!! happy though dangerous time away.

CHAPTER 6

Vice Admiral H.T. Baillie Grohman

Details

This account is taken from Admiral Grohman's personal papers which are held in the Imperial War Museum. He trained as a cadet aboard the HMS *Britannia*. He served aboard the cruiser, HMS *Grafton*, the flagship of the British navy's Pacific Fleet from September 1904 to 1905. From 1905 to 1907, he served aboard the flagship of the Atlantic Fleet, the HMS *Edward VII*, which was often based at Castletown Berehaven. Grohman witnessed the beginning of the 'Second Revolution' in China in 1913, while serving on the HMS *Monmouth*. He was based on the HMS *Lively* at Devonport at the outbreak of the First World War, the *Lively* joined the 7th Destroyer Flotilla, seeing action during the German raid on Great Yarmouth. During the War, he also served on the destroyer, HMS *Gurkha*, the minesweeper, HMS *Gentian*, and the minesweeper, HMS *Totnes*. During the War of Independence, he served aboard the HMS *Truro*, a minesweeper based in Portland, which was employed in fishery protection duties. It was also based in Cobh, and acted as a support to coastguard stations, and to prevent smuggling.

Ireland 1920 to 1921

SERIOUS REBELLION IN Ireland raised its head again in 1919 to 1921.
My ship the *Truro* had two spells of service there together with
three others of the Minesweeping Flotilla in 1920/21. With a number of destroyers, we were based at Queenstown (now called Cobh)
then the British naval base in Ireland. It is a really beautiful harbour with lovely country round it. Of course there was no Eire then,
and all Ireland was as much part of the United Kingdom as Scotland
and Wales.

144,000 Irishmen had voluntarily joined our armies in the First
World War and the Navy had always Irish recruits. Nevertheless,
during a most critical period for us in the First World War, some Irish
rebels known as Sinn Féiners, raised a rebellion in Dublin later to be
known as Easter Rising 1916. It was later estimated that there were
not more than 2,000 of these rebels. They were known to be in
touch with the Germans from whom shiploads of arms were
expected. These were intercepted by the Navy. In this rising some
100 British troops were killed in the street fighting and 200
wounded. Moreover a number of British officers and their wives murdered at night in a most cold blooded way, while asleep in various
hotels. Much damage to Dublin was done. The rebellion was put
down, and ten rebels were executed, but the trouble simmered on.

The Irish called the 1919-21 'trouble' the Anglo-Irish War
and their early policy was to ruthlessly murder isolated units of
the Irish Constabulary but eventually matters got worse, murder, arson, troops ambushed or attacked individually and so on.
But as far as I could ascertain then or since, no Naval officer or
man had been in any way attacked. It was the Irish
Constabulary, our Army, and any civilians who supported them
in any way who were the targets. Eventually the British sent to
Ireland auxiliaries who became known as the Black and Tans to
keep order, they became exceedingly unpopular with the Irish.

In Belfast, there were many shootings and ruthless murders between July 1920 and July 1921. Many of the Catholic clergy supported the so called Anglo-Irish War, whose object was a completely independent Ireland. Over the centuries, the British has resisted this, fearing to have an enemy on our flank, possibly supported by a European country, and one moreover so situated geographically as to be able to control our essential sea lanes and so our destiny.

The result of this trouble was the Anglo-Irish Treaty of December 1921, which gave all Ireland Dominion Status, with Ulster given the right to opt out, and remain part of the United Kingdom while Great Britain reserved the right to keep certain ports in Ireland including Queenstown, Berehaven and Loch Swilly. This right was given up by our Prime Minister Neville Chamberlain in December 1938, to the surprise of the Irish Government, as a gesture to the Nazis, thereby greatly handicapping us in the protection of shipping in the Second World War and costing hundreds of lives and many ships.

However, once this settlement of December 1921 was made, a terrible and most destructive civil war broke out in Ireland against the new Irish Government – Irishman v Irishman. This was a worse trouble for Ireland than the previous one. How the Irish love a fight! As before, this too often deteriorated into cold blooded murder.

The Irish Government forces took a year to put it down, and at the end of 1923 the worst was over and the Government had some 70,000 prisoners on their hands and 70 executions had been carried out by them in this year.

The main job for the Navy during my first spell there in 1920 was to help maintain the coastguard stations and the lighthouses round the coast of which there were a large number. The crews had been sent to Coventry by the Sinn Féiners, and no-one dared contact them in any way or keep them supplied. Incidentally, the great majority of the men in the coastguard stations were Irishmen who had served in the Navy, but this made no difference to their treatment by the Sinn Féiners.

There were many of these stations, some exposed to the full force of the Atlantic weather and others tucked away in sheltered coves and inlets, the sort of place where smugglers might want to land, and which the CG St. were there to prevent.

My ship had quite inadequate boats for this sort of work. Two clumsy 20 foot merchant type 4 oared gigs, one small dinghy and no power boat. It was tough going at times to land on the weatherbeaten coasts. Some of our charts of the Irish coasts were old, some dated 1840. Leading marks given had often disappeared and shoals shifted. This did not exactly help matters.

For a period I had two Rear Admirals on board, Rear Admiral Somerville, the Rear Admiral in charge of Coastguards for Southern Ireland and Rear Admiral Glossop who was taking over his appointment. The plan was to inspect all coastguard stations from Dublin southabout to Galway, and *Truro* was selected to take them. It was quite a job, I had no Navigator, and would have to do it all by myself.

All went well at first on board, but unfortunately the two flag officers started a fierce quarrel between themselves. Apparently, a British Army officer had been travelling in plain clothes by train from the North of Ireland to the South. He was in a railway carriage with five or six other travellers, when, at a small railway station, the Sinn Féiners searched the train for someone they wanted, and one could guess pretty certainly that, if found, he would be murdered – such were the times.

It was the British Army officer they were after. He was taken off the train at pistol point, without any protest or resistance from the other occupants or passengers, and before the train started again, the volley ending his life was heard. Glossop – new to the country – took the attitude that it was most cowardly of the Irish and the other occupants of the carriages not to resist. Somerville – an old hand and Irish – strongly disagreed and insisted it would have been useless. So for some days there was an embarrassing time, especially when each Flag Officer in turn came to me separately and gave me his views on the matter. However they calmed down after an interval.

I recollect Rear Admiral Glossop, although he had been a Navigator himself was a great nuisance on the bridge when entering or leaving harbour for he would place himself bang in front of the standard compass. (I should mention he was Captain of the cruiser *Sydney*, which sank the German raider *Emden* early in the war.) I wonder how many coastguard stations we visited. Was it thirty or could it have been more? At this distance of time I can't remember. I was some weeks in this job and really enjoyed it.

It was anxious navigation for me at times into the harbours, but we survived! Sailing directions and charts were old and out of date.

During this time I had much contact with the Army both on the shore and when military parties took passage in my ship. Several officers told me of the obscene mutilations carried out on dead British soldiers after an ambush or attack. These they had themselves seen, it was no yarn. They could not believe that any Irishman could commit such atrocities and put these mutilations down to gangsters over from Chicago or New York. There were rumours that many had come over.

On one occasion, I had just anchored off Youghal on the South coast when a loud explosion occurred on the shore not far from the town where a newly arrived Regiment (Scotch I believe) was stationed. There was a rifle range outside the town, to which the troops marched twice a week with bands playing. On this occasion, a land mine had been exploded under the troops on the march with heavy casualties especially amongst the band. An electric lead was traced to a nearby haystack where two women were hiding. The previous regiment had been a Yorkshire one (if I remember rightly) and there had been no trouble and a very friendly attitude in the neighbourhood. The Colonel of this regiment, however, always took precautions, for instance when marching to the rifle range, he had scouts ahead and on the flanks. He told the Scotch Colonel, who, however, in view of the absence of trouble so far adopted the policy of not showing suspicion, with this deplorable result. When I came on the scene within an hour of the explosion I found a sad and bloody spectacle on the road. Most of the victims were young bandsmen. I have forgotten what the exact casualties were.

Another time I was sent from Queenstown to Fishguard to fetch the Public Executioner and his assistant. I remember my sailing orders stated something to the effect that I was to remember he was a high state official and was to be treated accordingly, so he and his black bag, which I imagine contained ropes, and the Sub-Lieutenant's cabin during the passage. We had foul weather and he and his assistant were very seasick. On arrival at Queenstown these two, both looking like death itself (appropriately enough) and the bag were transferred to a launch which was heavily escorted, and were taken to Cork where the jail was. However, that evening the three men were pardoned, and another ship took the Lord High Executioner back to Fishguard. He was the type of man one would not be surprised to find as the landlord of a good public house – perhaps he was.

After five or six months in Ireland I had a spell at Portland but returned to Ireland for much of the winter and spring of 1921. I found the policy for the coastguard stations had been changed and it had been decided to evacuate them, and my ship was one of those so employed. It was not always easy owing to the weather and my clumsy and unsuitable boats. The southwest and west coasts of Ireland are not exactly millponds in the winter and spring. We had to take on board not only families, personal luggage and family treasures but furniture, pets, including donkeys at times and all sorts of coastguard flags and stores.

Sometimes we started the job in reasonable weather, which would then change, or a heavy swell would intervene, holding up the rest of the operations perhaps for some days while the ship with two anchors down and much cable veered, rolled and pitched. Sometimes it was best to get underway and patrol till weather subsided!

I was sent to Waterford several times to bring to Queenstown private firearms, for an order had been issued that private arms were to be handed in to prevent the rebels seizing them. Waterford was a collection depot. There were severe penalties for not complying.

The approach to Waterford by sea is a lovely one as is the town's waterfront. I lay alongside there and made an official call on the Mayor which he duly returned. He told me that during the World War that if a man wanted to join the British Army, and quite a number did, he had to smuggle himself out of the country. But if he was going to join the Royal Navy all honour to him and he was played out, so to speak, 'with guard and band'.

Some 300 or so private weapons were brought on board on these occasions. They were an interesting and varied collection. There would be for instance a pair of Purdey guns belonging to Lord Somebody, right down to the roughest possible weapons such as metal tubes or pipes lashed by wire to chocks of wood as a butt barely shaped by an axe.

One visitor I had on board was the owner of three small drapery shops along the coast. He was convinced that by refusing to buy British goods to store his shops he could seriously injure Britain's economy.

During this term of duty we were warned by the Admiral that the Sinn Féiners were plotting to capture a ship flying the White Ensign. I was naturally determined it would not be my ship that would fall into their hands, and made suitable arrangements. Once at anchor in Castletownsend, large fishing boats passed close under my stern on their way to and from the entrance. Each could hold 40 or 50 men and the situation could be awkward if say four or more of them suddenly put their helm up and ran alongside me. If unready my crew of 70 could have been swamped by numbers. My preparations on board included machine guns and rifles each side of the fore bridge always manned, strong nets to prevent boarding at certain points and steel flexible hose pipes led to the upper deck direct from the boilers to pour scalding steam on any attackers. But no attempt was made. I must say I was disappointed!

While in this harbour I gave leave up to 7pm but once two men did not return until 24 hours later. They had been taken by Sinn Féiners in a pub and taken to a barn outside the town for the night where they overheard their guards planning an attack on the *Truro*. They managed to escape and brought the news.

By a strange coincidence, while I was writing this 51 years later, the IRA were seizing and blowing up two small Naval Survey launches in Baltimore Harbour, not far from Castletownsend.

I paid several visits to Castletownsend, a charming port and got to know Miss Somerville, the author of many very amusing Irish books.

Near this harbour was an offshore lighthouse (I forget its name) but one night when I was passing the usual flashing light was not shown and several red rockets went up from it. I anchored nearby and sent an officer and small party to investigate. It appeared that the Sinn Féiners had attacked the lighthouse earlier that evening and stolen the gunpowder (or explosive whatever it was they used for fog signals) put the light out of action and on departing had locked the entrance which we had to break open.

On my return passage to Portland I gave a passage to a newly joined Naval cadet, Somerville by name. Later in 1940 my son, Michael, served in his destroyer in the Mediterranean and I met him again. He was killed in Malta in April 1941 when a bomb burst at the entrance to an air raid shelter, my son escaping this fate as he had temporarily gone back to his destroyer, which was in dry dock. Somerville was looked upon as being in the front rank of our many fine destroyer officers at this time.

By this time my service in Ireland was over in 1921, I was looking forward to a year at the RN Staff College at Greenwich. My wife and I had had a very spasmodic and scanty homelife at Rodwell, and it was high time this changed, especially with the two boys growing up.

Chapter 7

Captain R.D. Jeune

Details

This account was written in 1972 is taken from the private papers of Captain Jeune held in the Imperial War Museum. During the First World War, Jeune served as an interpreter with the 1st Indian Cavalry Division in France from September 1914 to September 1915. He commanded the 94th Trench Mortar Company, from October 1915 to October 1916, seeing service at the Battle of the Somme. He also commanded the 24th Trench Mortar Battery in the Ypres Salient from June to July 1917. He took part in the British Military Mission in Poland, from January 1919 to December 1920. Afterwards he served in intelligence duties in Ireland, mainly in Dublin, where he served alongside the Cario Gang. He was one of the few British Intelligence Officers to survive Bloody Sunday.

DURING THE SUMMER of 1972, I made the acquaintance of Mr. T.E. Utley, of the *Daily Telegraph*, who had written a very sound article on the Ulster question. I had asked him whether he would be interested to know what really happened in Dublin during the Sinn Féin Troubles in 1920-21. He said that he would be very interested and asked me to write an account of my experiences there, which I did. He has, I understand, been trying to find a means of getting it published, but after meeting him several times I have heard nothing more.

Herewith, therefore, a copy, in case anybody may be interested.

A very considerable degree of optimism would be required by anyone seeking to analyse and appreciate the complexities of the Irish question. Add to the political aspect, the religious, plus the historical, the climatic laziness, and to these the rebellious Irish temperament, and the result is a mixture capable of defying the probing of the most determined psycho-analyst. Some clarification may possibly be derived from referring to the failure of the Romans to exercise their civilising influence in Ireland. Likewise to misunderstanding and some misrule, or lack of rule, from Whitehall and to absentee landlordism. So is it surprising that there have been many troublous times in the Emerald Isle?

In considering the present crisis in Ulster, it may be of interest to recall the situation in Dublin in 1920-21, and to note the similarities and differences.

Those of us whose memories are long enough will remember the loyalty shown by the people of Ulster, the gallant record of the 36th Ulster Division, which suffered such grievous loses at Thiepval on 1st July, 1916. On the other hand there was the Easter 1916 rising in Dublin, which stabbed us in the back though it must not be forgotten that many Southern Irish fought with us.

After the rising had been crushed, possibly with rather excessive harshness, resistance simmered, being punctuated by occasional raids on police stations, the murder of some police and Residential Magistrates, until it was realised in Whitehall that this had to stop. A rather hastily improvised Intelligence Organisation was formed, of which I was a member, and after a short course of instruction at Hounslow, we were sent over to Dublin in the early summer of 1920.

The first batch were instructed to pose, initially, as RE officers, but this rather futile procedure was soon dropped and the work consisted of getting to know the town thoroughly, tailing 'Shinners', and carrying out small raids, with a view to collecting all possible information which would lead us eventually to stamping out the revolt.

For example, I received orders to carry out a surreptitious night raid on the house of Arthur Griffith, the self-styled Vice-President of the Irish Republic. A successful and unobserved entry was effected, and a number of subversive documents were removed, which proved to be of considerable interest.

On the following day, the local press published a report stating Mr Griffith's house had been raided by 'expert Cracksmen'!

At that time, the general situation in Dublin was quite normal on the surface, and quite different from that prevailing at present in Ulster. There was no bombing or shooting, and, of course, no internecine religious strife, though in the country districts the number of cases of illicit drilling, burning of country houses, attacks on police stations and shooting of police officers was mounting. In this context, the often misunderstood and misapplied term 'Black and Tan' should be mentioned. During and shortly after the war, losses to the Royal Irish Constabulary were sometimes replaced by recruits from England. The uniform of the RIC was a dark green tunic and black trousers. Owing to the difficulty of supplying sufficient green tunics, the recruits were fitted out with khaki jackets, and were consequently known as the Black and Tans, after the well-known Irish pack of hounds. Incidentally, in 1919 a few couple of these hounds were bought by the Cotswold Hunt.

Later, in the summer of 1920 a new police force was raised, composed of British ex-officers, and known as the Auxiliary Police Force. They wore khaki uniform with Glengarry caps, and were housed in barracks. Mistakenly the term 'Black and Tan' came to be applied to them. We often collaborated with them; and there was no nonsense with the IRA.

In September 1920, a raid took place, which had a significant result. It was decided to raid several houses in Drumcondra, and that we were to have the help of a detachment of the East Lancs. Particular attention was attached to the house of a man called O'Connor, known to us as an active Sinn Féiner. At the arranged signal I charged the door, but it did not give, so I charged again, and this time it flew open, and, much to the amusement of the Tommies, I went slithering along the linoleum-covered floor on my front.

There was no hostile reception, however, and the search went on. While this was happening I was standing talking to Boddington, who was in charge of the raid, then a letter was brought to him, which he read and handed to me, saying: 'Money for jam.' It was on official Dublin Castle paper and was in these words:

Dear Mr. O'Connor,
I am having the papers you require sent to you.
Yours Sincerely,
A.W. Cope

This was distinctly interesting. Here was the Assistant Under Secretary writing to a notorious Sinn Féiner, with whom he had obviously already been in contact.

After this I made a point of trying to find out more about this individual's doings, and found that he had done some rather strange things, such as arranging for some electricians of known Sinn Féin views to come into the Castle at unusual times. Also he was one of the very few Castle officials who could safely walk about the streets of Dublin. But it was decided that no drastic action could be taken against him, as it turned out that he was a protégé of Lloyd-George, who had picked him out of the Fisheries and sent him over to

Ireland under Sir John Anderson in order to get a foot in the Sinn Féin camp, or, in modern parlance, to set in motion an 'initiative'. Later he was given a good job in the Liberal Party.

A little later, in October, we were involved in a disastrous raid, also in Drumcondra. Shortly before, Col. Smyth had been murdered in the County Club in Cork by Dan Breen, the leader of the original murder gang, which also included Sean Tracey, Denis Lacey and Sean Hogan. Major Smyth had come from India to avenge his brother's murder, and he asked if he could join us, so, when it was decided to visit some houses where it was thought that wanted men were given shelter, about half a dozen of us, including Major Smyth, set out at night in a truck to investigate a house near Kingstown (now called, Dun Laoghaire). But we drew a blank, so we went on chance to Professor Carolan's house, Fernside, Drumcondra.

As was our custom, my immediate chief, Phil Attwood, and I went round to the back of the house and waited in the garden. Suddenly we heard a volley of shots in the house, and Phil said to me 'Come on Bob, let's go in'. This seemed the natural thing to do, but it turned out to be a grievous mistake. At the back of the house was a conservatory, and as I went in I saw Michael, whose surname I have forgotten, raise his pistol and fire a couple of shots. I asked him what he was firing at, and he said, 'He came down from the window and I think I got him in the leg. He has gone up again'. It was obvious that the only way then to get back into the garden to prevent any escape was to go by the same way by which we had originally gone, so I ran round the house, but by the time I had got back into the garden it was too late, and there was no sign of my gunmen.

What had happened in the house was that Major Smyth had opened the door of the back bedroom and walked in, with a torch alight on his belt. All the gunman, who turned out later to have been Dan Breen had to do was to shoot Smyth through the heart. At this there was some confusion, during which Captain White, a very nice man with an excellent war record, was killed, and Cpl. Worth wounded. A little later, from the garden, I heard a single shot, which made one think that there might still be a gunman in the house. But, far from that, it was a most unfortunate accident, which involved Professor Carolan being shot by mistake while being questioned. He was taken to hospital, but died some weeks later.

In 1924 Dan Breen published his memoirs in a book called *My fight for Irish Freedom*, a copy of which was sent to me by one of my former colleagues. In it Dan Breen gives a highly imaginative account, full of flagrant lies, of this affair. He gives details, and these may well be true of his escape and of the time he spent in the Mater Hospital and other places, until he was able to resume his activities. Incidentally he seems, strangely enough, not to have been proud of having murdered Colonel Smyth in the County Club, Cork, because he just records – 'He was shot dead in the County Club in the heart of Cork City'.

After this, the situation was clearly hotting up. Sean Tracey, who had been with Dan Breen at Fernside, was shot in an affray in Talbot Street, and other gunmen were captured. During all this time, Michael Collins, the head of the IRA, was at large. There was a high price on his head, but he seemed to led a charmed life, enjoying many narrow escapes from death or capture, until he was eventually killed in an ambush during the civil war after the Treaty.

In November, information was coming in well and we were beginning to get on top of the IRA, who were becoming desperate. I happened to receive information from three different sources to the effect that something was going to happen, but there was nothing definite.

In the evening of Saturday 20 November, I received orders to collect my fellows and search the railway yards at Inchicore, where it was thought that ammunition might be stored. We went there and searched for several hours, but there was obviously nothing to be found, so we slept in railway carriages, and in the morning I telephoned the Castle and asked whether I was to be relieved. Our Adjutant, Hyems, said 'I am sorry to say that there have been some raids by the "Shinners" and I am afraid that they have got some of our fellows'. So it was agreed that we should return to our lodgings. I was at that time sharing a flat at 28 Upper Pembroke Street, with a colleague, Murray, and on getting back there I found a very distressing scene.

In the flat next to Murray's and mine, I saw the body of my friend 'Chummy' Dowling, a grand ex-guardee, wounded three times in the war, lying full length on the floor. As he was to have relieved me he was in uniform and had obviously been shot through the heart, probably by a small Sinn Féiner because there was a bullet hole in one corner of the ceiling. In the doorway of the bathroom was Price's body. Murray had already been taken to hospital. Colonel Woodcock, commanding the 1st East Lancs, had been shot three times, but survived. Likewise Captain Keenleyside, Adjutant of the same battalion. Colonel Montgomery had been shot on the stairs, as he came up after breakfast. He died some time later. Mrs Woodcock wrote a full account of all this in *Blackwood's Magazine* a few months later.

In addition, Peter Ames and Bennett, who had been in 28 Upper Pembroke Street, the evening before when I went out, were murdered in their beds in Lower Leeson Street. Two officers, temporarily at the Gresham Hotel, while going on leave, or returning, I think, were also shot dead. Two or three gunmen were shot and captured in another street.

In the afternoon we received information to the effect that the gunmen had been told to meet at Croke Park, where a football match was to be played that afternoon, in order to compare notes. I was not in on this, but saw a number of truckloads of police moving off, and was told later that, when they arrived at

Croke Park, they were fired on, and of course opened fire, causing a number of casualties.

After the crowd had dispersed, the police found a considerable number of revolvers and automatic pistols on the ground.

The object of this exercise on the part of the IRA, was to eliminate Intelligence and Courts Martial officers, because the gunmen felt that the net was closing round them. So men were brought up to Dublin from other parts of the country, particularly Tipperary, in order to catch as many as possible of us unawares on a Sunday morning, when most people slept late.

As a result of all this, those of us who had survived were shut up under guard in a hotel, from where it was impracticable to do any useful work. In fact, our job had to all intents and purposes been done, and the organisation was breaking up.

So at about the New Year I applied for leave, and on the boat met General Boyd, GOC Dublin District, with whom I used to play tennis on the Castle courts. He said 'Well, Jeune, I think we have broken the back of the movement now, don't you?' I replied 'Yes, sir, and I think six months should see it out', to which he answered 'Yes, I think you are right. Hamar Greenwood (then Colonial Secretary, and in charge of Irish affairs) says two months, but I think that is rather optimistic'.

This, as stated, was about the New Year 1921, and by the early summer the IRA were driven into the south west corner of Ireland, and would have been quickly finished. But certain influences were to save them, as I learned later in London from a friend of mine, Jeffries, who had been in our show in Dublin. When this broke up he, with a staff officer, Cameron, were instructed to set up from London a proper secret service in Ireland, which was very successfully accomplished.

About this time De Valera came back from the USA and was captured in a raid by Lord Twining, then a young subaltern in the

Worcesters, whom I met in London a few years ago, not long before his death. He told me that he did not know the identity of his prisoner, who at first would not give his correct name, but did so eventually.

Now Jeffries told me that the following took place. Army GHQ at Kilmainham wired to his London office 'De Valera captured. Cope suggests release'. This telegram arrived about 7pm and Jeffries took it across to the Colonial Office, but Hamar Greenwood had left, so Jeffries took it to Lloyd-George, who rubbed his hands together, and said 'Well done the military. He must on no account be released'. Taking this as settled, Jeffries left, but as soon as he had gone Lloyd-George sent orders for De Valera to be released, which was done.

Later, yielding to threats from the IRA, Lloyd-George agreed to meet a delegation headed by Michael Collins, with a view to drawing up a treaty. At this time, as may well be remembered, Field-Marshal Sir Henry Wilson, a distinguished Ulsterman, was invited by Lloyd-George to join him and one or two other politicians in meeting the Irish delegation. He replied, saying that he had no intention of 'seeing three bloody murderers dictating to three damned cowards'. He was murdered in Eaton Square, by two ex-soldiers, acting on orders, from the IRA.

The Treaty was signed. The IRA had won. Does history repeat itself?

CHAPTER 8

Lieutenant General A.E. Percival

Details

This account is taken from two lectures given by Percival, copies
of which are not held in his private papers at the Imperial War
Museum. Percival joined the Essex Regiment as a temporary second lieutenant in September 1914, and was appointed a temporary
Lieutenant in October 1914, and a temporary Captain in November
1914. By 1917, he was a temporary Lieutenant Colonel, commanding the 7th Battalion Bedfordshire Regiment. During the First
World War, he also held battalion command of an Essex Battalion
and of a battalion of the Bedfordshire & Hertfordshire Regiment.
He served in Russia in 1919, as a Major with the Royal Fusiliers, and
returned to the Essex Regiment for service in Ireland from 1919 to
1921. He later served with the Cheshire Regiment during 1924. From
1925 to 1929, he served with the Royal West African Frontier Force,
returning to the Cheshire Regiment in 1929. He taught at the Staff
College, Camberley, from 1931 to 1932. From 1936 to 1938, he served
in Malaya, as a General Staff Officer, Grade 1, returning in 1938 to
England to Staff Command at Aldershot as a Brigader-General.
During World War Two, Percival served as a Brigadier with 1st
Corps BEF in France from 1939 to 1940. He served also in 1940 as

Assistant Chief of Imperial Staff. He was appointed as GOC Malaya in July 1941, and as the commander of British forces at Singapore surrendered the city to the Japanese Army in 1942, and was imprisoned in Manchuria for the remainder of the Second World War. He retired in 1946.

Guerrilla Warfare, Ireland 1920-1921
Introduction

MY OBJECT IN the two lectures which I am going to give you on Guerrilla warfare in Ireland during 1920 and 1921 is firstly to give those of you who did not take part in the Irish War, an idea of the conditions prevailing there and of the various problems with which we as soldiers were confronted and, secondly, to explain to you how we solved these problems, and to give you the reasons which influenced our solutions. The problems I shall deal with will be in the main tactical problems, and I shall, as far as possible, avoid all political and religious questions, though it will be necessary to touch on these briefly as they had such an important influence on the conduct of military operations.

In my first lecture I propose to give you a general outline of the conditions prevailing in the South of Ireland at the commencement of 1920, and then to trace step by step the evolution of the struggle from that date till the Spring of 1921. I shall deal with the various problems as they arose and explain to you how they were influenced by changing conditions.

In my second lecture, I shall deal with the operations during the final period (April-July 1921) and shall give you my conclusions as to the best methods to be employed in warfare of this nature. I shall also deal with the organisation of intelligence within the battalion – a very important subject – and shall conclude with what I consider were some of the outstanding lessons from a military point of view.

Personal Experiences
In the course of my lecture I shall give you a few personal experiences; this I shall do, not in any spirit of self-aggrandisement, but purely with a view to illustrating the type of warfare in which we were engaged.

Appointments held and Area dealt with
I went to Ireland in January 1920 and served with my Regiment there till the Truce. The Battalion was stationed at Kinsale with a number of outlying Detachments, and was responsible for a large tract of country in west Cork, probably one of the most disturbed areas in the whole of Ireland. I was first placed in command of the Bandon Detachment and was subsequently given a special position as Intelligence Officer and organiser of operations in the battalion area.

General Description of Country
I will now give you a short description of the conditions which prevailed in County Cork at the beginning of 1920.

The country is generally wild with large uncultivated tracts. There are a few small towns e.g. Kinsale, Bandon, Clonakilty, Bantry and Macroom and a number of villages, mostly situated in the valleys between the hills. The industry of the country is almost entirely agricultural, the land being divided up into small farms, most of which are owned by the farmers themselves, or in the process of passing into their possession under the terms of the Wyndham Land Act of 1903.

There are, therefore, a number of farmhouses scattered all over the countryside. The fields are invariably small and divided from each other by stone walls with furze growing on top, which makes the range of vision very restricted. In the Bandon and Kinsale district a fairly large proportion of the land is under cultivation, but

Lieutenant General Percival (right), then a major, pictured in the company of a senior RIC officer in Bandon Barracks, County Cork.

further to the west and north-west the country becomes very wild and hilly, consisting chiefly of bogs and gorse-covered hillsides with small homesteads tucked away here and there on the sides of the hills.

Roads

The main roads between the towns are fairly good and suitable for all traffic: some of the country roads, however, are very rough and in many places the inclines are very steep; they are nearly passable for HT and light lorries, but not for 3-ton lorries. Thus the main convoy lorry routes were very restricted.

Railways

There is one main railway the Cork, Bandon, and South Coast, which runs westward from Cork to Bantry, branch lines run southward from this to Kinsale, Clonakilty and Skibbereen.

Rivers

The Bandon River rises in the hills north-east of Bantry, and after flowing due east through Bandon, turns sharply south till it reaches the sea at Kinsale; the few bridges which exist over this river very much restrict the choice of alternative routes when moving from one locality to another. The country is intersected by a number of small streams, which, though in themselves no obstacle, necessitate a large number of bridges which facilitate the blocking of the roads.

The Population

The inhabitants of this country were clearly divided into different parties, whose sympathies and interests were diametrically opposed.

The Old Landlords

Only a few of these remained, the majority of them living in large

A joint Army and RIC patrol leave Limerick on a reconnaissance mission, 1920.

houses with only a little land attached, the rest of their property having passed to the tenant farmers under the Wyndham Land Act. As will be seen later, they were, however, an important factor in the situation. They had English sympathy but avoided active participation.

The Protestant Element
Chiefly large farmers and shop-keepers. They were practically unanimously in favour of a continuation of English control in the south, but they had no organisation of their own, and were not armed; they were, therefore, powerless against the attacks of Sinn Féin. A few, but not many, were brave enough to assist Crown Forces with information.

The Priests
The Catholic priests could be divided into two categories – the elderly men, who had formally been the leaders of the people, but had recently lost all control, and the young priests who had passed through Maynooth College and were thoroughly imbued with Republican principles; the latter were almost without exception heart and soul in the Sinn Féin movement.

The Catholic Population
Finally there was the Catholic population, the large majority of which, if not active Sinn Féins, were sympathic to the Sinn Féin movement. The extent of their activity usually varied in the inverse ratio to their financial interest in the country – they were, for instance, the farmers and large shopkeepers who disliked disturbances, and the farmers' sons and corner boys, who had no stake in the country and preferred earning a living by plunder and murder than by doing an honest day's work. There were a large number of this latter class owing to the failure of the British Government to enforce conscription in Southern Ireland during the war, and they

A group of suspected IRA volunteers are photographed after being captured by the Essex Regiment during operations in west Cork.

nearly all had an exaggerated idea of their own importance. It was of these men that the Republican Army was mainly composed.

Sinn Féin

The Sinn Féin movement, which started in 1905 was originally moderate in character, aiming at the commercial prosperity of Ireland, and the regaining of political independence. Later it got into the hands of extremists, such as the Irish Republican Brotherhood and when the war broke out began the plot with Germany. It received a setback in 1916, when the Dublin rebellion was stamped out, but quickly set to work to collect money again, which was plentiful in the country owing to the boom in farming during the latter part of the war. After their victory at the General Election in 1918, the Sinn Féin extremists worked steadily with one end in view, viz: the formation of an Independent Republic. This they did by filling the Local Government, Councils etc. with their own members, setting up their own courts, and enforcing their will by means of the Irish Republican Army.

The point I want to make here is that the rebel campaign in Ireland was a national movement backed by a large proportion of the population and was not conducted by a few hired assassins as was often supposed.

The Irish Republican Army

The organisation of the Irish Republican Army was much more complete than was generally known; it was organised on a Territorial basis with the Brigade the highest formation, Division only been formed at a later date. A Bde. Consisted of from four to seven Battalions and a Battalion of any number of COs up to ten. Generally speaking each village or townland provided a CO, this arrangement facilitating training and circulation of orders, etc. The strength of the COs varied considerably, but 50-60 could be taken as a general average.

A joint patrol of cyclists from the Essex Regiment and members of the RIC pose for a photograph prior to going out on patrol from Bandon, County Cork.

The officers were generally selected from the most desperate men of the neighbourhood, the rank and file consisting chiefly of labourers and young recruits.

A few of the officers had uniforms, but these were only worn when they did not expect to come in contact with the Crown Forces. There were, however, secret signs in the IRA by which an officer could be distinguished; for instance, they usually wore brown leggings while the rank and file wore black ones, etc. There was, however, outwardly nothing to distinguish a member of the IRA from any ordinary member of the community. This of course assisted them enormously in their operations as they could at any moment convert themselves from an armed soldier into a peaceful civilian, whose identity it would be exceedingly difficult to establish.

The arms in possession of the IRA were of a very mixed assortment, ranging from old fashioned shot guns firing slugs, to the modern Thompson Light Automatic with a rate of fire of 700 rounds a minute. On an average a Company would have six or seven service rifles, ten or twelve revolvers, a number of shotguns and occasionally a Light Automatic Weapon. Their ammunition supply for this varied assortment of weapons was, of course, very difficult and their plans had to be laid in accordance with the amount of ammunition available. This was one the reasons why they relied almost entirely on surprise action – ambushes etc. – rather that on larger engagements. They appeared, however, to get a fairly regular supply of Government pattern SAA .303. Some of this was captured by them in successful ambushes, while some was doubtless secretly imported from England.

The training of the IRA was carried out entirely in secret, Company parades often taking place in some isolated spot on Sunday afternoons. On these occasions the surrounding hills would be carefully picquetted with scouts, which made it very difficult for the Crown Forces to approach the 'parade ground' unseen.

Belgooly RIC Barracks near Kinsale, County Cork, after it was mined by the IRA during an attack.

The IRA Intelligence Service was, of course, easy owing to the majority of the population being friendly, but nevertheless it reached a very high standard of efficiency, and every movement, and very often every intended movement, of the Crown Forces was known; information was passed about in an uncanny sort of way without any organisation being apparent on the surface.

In consequence of this, it was essential for the utmost secrecy to be maintained in the preparation of plans for military operation and especially in the arrangements for the movements either of troops or of individuals. I found from personal experience that it was fatal to issue orders for any operation more than an hour or two before the troops were due to start, and then the plan should be known only to one or two necessary officers before the troops actually paraded. It is impossible in work of this kind to prevent soldiers and very often even officers, from prejudicing the chances of success of a whole operation by one or two unguarded remarks.

Communications

Owing to the constant searches carried out by the Crown Forces, it was exceedingly difficult for the IRA to issue anything in the way of written orders, but they did succeed, in spite of these difficulties, in an extraordinary way of getting their orders circulated. This they did largely by verbal instructions issued at fixed meeting places – often in selected farmhouses, public houses, etc. and it was these meeting places which it was one of our main objects to find out and surprise.

Operations were discussed and planned at a meeting of the Brigade Council, which was usually held fortnightly, the meeting place being changed each time. At the meeting battalion commanders were present and received their instructions for forthcoming operation.

Women were employed largely for carrying messages and orders about, and as these could only be searched by 'women searchers',

Suspects in the murder of Sergeant Mulhern being marched into Bandon Barracks by a patrol from the Essex Regiment, July 1920.

who were not often available when required, it will be seen that the IRA 'Lines of communications' were not at all vulnerable.

The Crown Forces
I will now attempt to outline briefly the organisation of the Crown Forces during the period under review:

(a) The RIC
The Royal Irish Constabulary was organised by 'Districts' and 'Counties' with an officer or Inspector in charge of each. The 'County' included a number of 'Districts' and a 'District' usually consisted of a 'District Headquaters', where the DI lived, and a number of outlying barracks, where about eight to twelve policemen lived under a Sergeant. Their duty was primarily the maintenance of law and order in their locality and it is clear that in these isolated posts, which were often eight or ten miles apart, they were not in a position to carry out offensive operations against the rebels. Previous to 1920 their 'moral' had been high, but owing to the continuous activities of the IRA against them during that year, and the lack of proper support, their morale, with very few exceptions, gave way and thereafter they were of little assistance except to act as local guides.

To increase their strength, a number of ex-soldiers were enlisted in England and drafted to the various local Barracks; these were nicknamed the 'Black and Tans'. They were generally a very fine lot of men, and would have done well under other conditions.

(b) The Military
The country was divided up into Divisional Brigade. and Battalion areas, each unit being responsible for the area allotted to it. These areas were usually much too large to control effectively – for instance – my own Battalion at the beginning of 1920 was responsible for an

The funeral of Corporal Maddox, who died on intelligence operations, in the company of Major Percival (his picked man), July 1920, on its way out from Bandon Barracks, County Cork.

area stretching from Queenstown to Castletownbere, a distance of approximately 100 miles in length, and the Battalion only had strength of about 600 men! These areas were subsequently reduced by the arrival of fresh Battalions, but even at the end our Battalion area stretched from Carrigaline on the east to Ballineen on the west, and from Crookstown on the north to the sea on the south – an area of 400 square miles.

Our Battalion headquarters was at Kinsale, but in consequence of the large area, it was necessary to form a number of Company Detachments; these were established at Queenstown, Bantry and Bandon, but the two former were handed over to other units early in 1920 and other detachments formed as will be seen later.

The duty of the military at this time was to act in 'Aid of the Civil Power', ie, to support the RIC with troops as required, especially when they were attempting to arrest some of the ringleaders of the Sinn Féin movement. The Military at this time had no authority to act alone except in the cases of emergency, but had always to be accompanied by a number of the RIC.

(c) The Auxiliaries

This body was formed in the summer of 1920 and, though affiliated to the RIC, they had an independent organisation under their own officers. They consisted entirely of ex-officers and worked by companies, each company being allotted a district to work in where the rebel organisation appeared to be strongest. They eventually came under the Military area commander for tactical purposes, and were of assistance in the taking over responsibilities for the parts of the Military areas, but their independent status did not always make for smooth working, and the old difficulty arose of a force being under one commander for tactical purposes and another for administrative.

I now come to a description of the struggle between the IRA

British troops attempt to cross a trench dug by the IRA. The digging of trenches became a typical tactic to disrupt British communications.

and the Crown Forces between January 1920 and April 1921, and I will divide this into three periods.

January – September 1920
The object of Sinn Féin at this time, as has been pointed out, was to take over all administrative control of the country and to overthrow all British authority. To enable them to do this, it was necessary to prevent the Crown Forces from interfering with their courts, Local Government meetings, etc. The Activities of the IRA were, therefore, directed at that time against the RIC as being the representatives of the British Government and the only force which knew sufficient about the local activities of Sinn Féin to be able to take action against them. At this time the IRA leaders undoubtedly wished to avoid contact with the military. Their activities took the form of attacks on RIC Barracks at night, murder of policemen and a boycott of the RIC, ie, all shopkeepers were warned not to supply them with goods under penalty of death.

The government retaliated during the early part of this period by the arrest of a selected number of the IRA leaders; these arrests were carried out at night by the police assisted by military, the greatest care had to be exercised in approaching the houses of the wanted men, as they immediately made off if they got warning of the approach of Crown Forces. Troops usually proceeded out in lorries, which were left a mile or so from the house to be raided.

In May 1920 the morale of the RIC was badly shaken by the release of all the men who had been arrested, as these men immediately returned to their homes and organised the murder of those members of the RIC who had been instrumental in effecting their arrests. Attacks on the RIC Barracks increased and were of almost nightly occurrence. It, therefore, became the chief duty of the Military to protect the police by sending out relief parties in lorries whenever news was received that a police barracks was being attacked. To

A Rolls Royce armoured car attempts to bypass an IRA trench near Carrignavar, County Cork, 10 June 1921.

enable this news to be received in time wireless sets were erected on all RIC Barracks and were of great value in transmitting information.

When organising an attack on a Barracks, however, the IRA invariably blocked all approaches by felling trees across the road, this work being carried out by labour impressed locally, and it was therefore practically impossible for the military parties to arrive in time to attack the IRA before they had made off. On the other hand they were not often successful in capturing a barracks except when they managed to get an explosive charge under the wall and blow them up.

In consequence of these continual attacks and the powerlessness of the few RIC in each barracks for offensive operations, a change of policy was decided on, and a number of the smaller barracks were closed down the men being concentrated on the larger barracks and, to assist them in their offensive operations, Military Detachments, usually of one or two platoons, were formed in the vicinity of each RIC barracks. The commander of these detachments had a considerable responsibility and also scope for initiative. It was during this period that the really systematic collection of military intelligence was commenced, which proved to be invaluable for the operations carried out the following year. All officers were instructed to patrol their district freely and to get to know the country and the inhabitants thoroughly.

The following is a good example of the sort of thing which happened during this period.

On Sunday 25 July, Sgt. Mulhern, the Crime Special Sergeant of the RIC at Bandon, was entering the Catholic Church for Mass, when two men stopped him in the porch and shot him dead. They then quietly walked off, and though a large part of the congregation had seen and no doubt recognised them, they one and all refused to give evidence as to their identity.

The following night, I took a picked man and proceeded to the

A British mobile column finds its way blocked by fallen trees. This tactic, along with trench-ng, were the IRA's main tactics in disrupting the use of roads by the British Army.

house of the local IRA leader, which was situated only about 500 yards from our barracks, with a view to watching it; on entering the garden a shot rang out and the man with me fell dead, shot through the head by a fellow armed with a shot-gun loaded with slugs; we had walked on to the top of an IRA picquet which was protecting the house.

At dawn the following morning we carried out a raid on the house of one of the local IRA leaders, hoping to find some of the gunmen there, but without success. The same evening, however, we again raided the same house and on this occasion we were met in the farmyard by two well-dressed men, who said they were on holiday from Dublin. After we had been talking to them for some time. I was informed by the Cpl. in charge of my patrol that he had noticed the man I was talking to slipping pieces of paper from his pocket into the hedge behind. On investigation we found papers, which proved that this man was an important officer in the IRA and further search disclosed a box hidden in a bank, which contained most valuable information about the local IRA organisation. The two men were subsequently proved to be the commandant of the local IRA battalion and his quartermaster, the two men who had doubtless organised the murder on the previous day.

During this period the troops carried out a great number of searches for arms, but usually without result. It is so easy in a country of this nature to hide arms and ammunition that it is almost impossible to find them and I am of the opinion that it is in reality a waste of time to carry out too many searches unless very definite information has been obtained.

Bloodhounds were used in the endeavour to track down the culprits after a police murder, but although they gave several very good 'runs', there was seldom a kill. The difficulty was to get the dog on the ground soon enough after the murder had been committed.

The Essex Regiment's new Flying Column enjoys a rest in the sunshine on a roadside in west Cork during the early summer of 1921.

October–December, 1920

About the commencement of October 1920, the IRA decided that they could no longer ignore the military, but must include them in their operations. With this end in view they decided to strengthen their forces by the formation of Flying Columns. These columns were composed of those men who were permanently 'on the run', ie, these who could not live at their homes for fear of being arrested and included, therefore, all the most desperate men in the IRA. A column consisted of about 25 men and moved about the country billetting on different farms – usually those occupied by Loyalist farmers. They were well armed and very mobile, travelling on bicycles or in light country carts, and used entirely for offensive operations. It was about this time that they first began to ambush military lorries, and I will describe to you one of the first of these ambushes that took place, in which I happened to be concerned.

One night early in October, I took out a party in two Crossley lorries (about sixteen men all told) to raid a village called Castletown, which lies to the northwest of Bandon. On the way we had to pass through another village called Newcestown, where we arrived about 10.15pm. Seeing the local 'pub' full of men, I stopped the cars and had it surrounded, but as we did so a man, who pretended to be drunk, got past the sentry at the back door, and slipped away. After searching the remainder who all gave false names, but who, I knew well, were really just the local Company returned from parade, and after finding no arms or documents on them, we continued out journey, but had not gone more than 300 or 400 yards when a heavy fire was opened on both cars from behind the hedge on the side of the road. The cars were, of course, silhouetted in the light made by the head-lamps and were an excellent target. After passing through the ambush I stopped the cars and counter-attacked the enemy, who, by this time, had retired across the next field, and of course, could not be seen in the dark.

Brigadier General Higginson personally interviews suspected members of the IRA during operations in the Clydagh Valley, County Cork.

The result of this small action was that we had two officers killed and three men wounded, while we had probably inflicted no damage on the enemy. It subsequently transpired that the man who escaped out of the back-door of the 'pub', was the commandant of the local Flying Column which had just been formed, and which was at the time billetted at a farm just outside the village. He had just time to get them into position while we were busy in the 'pub'. This man's name was John Hales, who subsequently became a Deputy of the Free State Parliament, and was himself murdered in Dublin about a year ago.

In November 1920 took place the murder of fifteen officers in Dublin in their bedrooms on a Sunday morning.

During this period the Military had no powers of retaliation and were entirely on the defensive. In the bad areas lorry convoys escorted by armoured cars had to be organised, to take supplies to the various detachments and this was practically the only means of communication between one detachment and another. In fact, the whole of the strength of the Army was taken up with defensive and protective measures; the Army was forced, by the role imposed upon it, to entirely violate the principle of 'offensive action', and 'Economy of Force'. Lorry convoy tactics became quite a little problem in itself. It soon became evident that lorry convoys must consist of not less than six lorries with a suitable escort. To avoid all being ambushed simultaneously, these lorries were divided into two or more groups, which moved at 300 or 400 yds interval. Part of the escort was placed in each group, the idea being that, if ambushed, the other group would stop and the escort counter-atack the ambushers.

Very strict discipline was required to prevent lorries closing up too near to each other, or individual lorries becoming detached owing to breakdowns, etc. Experiments were made with armour plating on lorries, but though useful for town work, it was found that the lorries

Suspected IRA volunteers are photographed for future identification in Bandon Barracks, County Cork.

became too heavy for work on the country roads. Most of the lorries were, however, provided with plating to protect the drivers. Armoured cars (heavy pattern) if available accompanied the conveys.

The effect of the defensive attitude of the Government was to greatly raise the 'morale' of the IRA which increased in strength and efficiency and so bad did conditions become that Martial Law had to be declared in the most disturbed parts of Southern Ireland – Cork – Kerry – etc., on 10 December 1920.

January-March 1921

The main results of the declaration of Martial Law were:-
Operations assumed a military aspect, the military henceforth were able to function by themselves and it was not necessary for the military to be accompanied by the RIC.

The RIC practically ceased to function except for ordinary routine business, e.g., granting of licences, etc., individually, they were of assistance for supplying local intelligence.

The military authorities took over the complete control of the county as far as the restoration of law and order was concerned. The principal steps taken by the GOC 6th Division to this were:

> *(i)* The setting up of summary courts in the Bn. areas which were presided over by officers specially detailed for this duty. These officers were empowered to pass a sentence of six months imprisonment or to award a fine up to £50.
> *(ii)* A standing Courts-Martial sat at Cork consisting entirely of special Courts-Martial officers. This Court dealt with the more serious cases.
> (iii) Drum-head Courts-Martial for dealing with Rebels caught with arms in their hands.
> *(iv)* Penalties for harbouring rebels, or for failing to report ambushes, etc., or giving a wrong name.

A British tank crushes a house in Dillon's Cross, Cork, as part of an official reprisal in January 1921.

(v) A restriction was put on the holding of Fairs and Markets in the more disturbed areas, as these provided opportunities for the IRA leaders to meet together and discuss plans.

(vi) To hamper the communication of the IRA, the use of motor cars, except by specially authorised persons, e.g. Doctors, etc. was forbidden. The use of bicycles was similarly prohibited.

(vii) A curfew was declared in certain bad areas. This was later extended to cover the whole of the Martial Law area and was of great assistance to the Military, as it meant that anybody out after the curfew was automatically a law-breaker.

In addition to the above, the policy of internment was introduced about this time, by which any man, who was known to be a leader in the IRA, could be interned without trial.

It was realised now that the only chance of success was to take offensive action against the IRA. To enable this to be done, it was necessary to economise forces by reducing the number of small detachments in existence and accordingly the detachments at Ballineen and Timoleague were withdrawn, those at Bandon and Clonakilty being retained to provide bases for operations, this not only made available a number of men for active operations, but also reduced the amount of mechanical transport required for the supply of these detachments, which about this time became a matter of considerable difficulty.

The offensive operations now instituted first of all took the form of area round-ups, on a large scale. The usual procedure was to select an area to be searched, study it carefully on a map, and allot definite farms or houses to each party of half a dozen men under an officer. The whole party would then leave barracks either in lorries or on foot in time to arrive on the ground at dawn and commence the search, either working inwards towards the centre of a

A Peerless armoured car of the type used in Ireland during the War of Independence. The officer is a captain in the Royal Artillery.

circle or driving the area towards a line of 'stops' put out to catch the 'runners'. As only officers were allowed to enter houses, a large number of officers were required for this work. The orders issued were for all young men to be collected and brought to a rendezvous where they were sorted out and those known to be active members of the IRA kept for internment. This 'sorting out' process was a difficult affair as the 'wanted' men invariably gave wrong names, and it required a very good intelligence service to find out who they really were. The result of these operations was to collect a number of the ordinary rank and file of the IRA, but the leaders usually managed to escape, which was not difficult to do in such a thick and intricate country. On one occasion a soldier fell into a covered hole containing five stolen motor cars without actually seeing it.

The reply of the IRA to these activities was to deny to us the use of roads by cutting deep trenches across them, or destroying bridges, this they did with impress labour on all roads except one or two selected main roads which they left open for the ordinary civilian traffic and also with a view to catching lorry convoys in ambushes on these roads.

The attacks on the Crown Forces increased in intensity and assumed larger proportions than before, as the Crown Forces increased the strength of their escort parties in view of probable ambushes and the IRA had accordingly to increase their attacking parties. The IRA also began to use road mines for blowing up the leading lorries in the ambushes.

A good instance of an encounter which took place about this time was the Upton Train Ambush. This was an attack made by about 50 of the IRA on a train at Upton Station, as they knew a mail escort of about a dozen soldiers would be travelling on this train. The attackers seized the train station buildings and opened fire on the train as it drew up to the platform. The attack was beaten off by the escort with the loss of one soldier killed and one wounded. One of the attackers was killed and one captured, and about eight civilians were killed or died of their wounds. The attackers, of course, always cleared off as soon as possible to avoid being caught by military reinforcements and they were great adepts in the art of disappearing quickly.

On this occasion, although we had a strong party from Bandon on the scene about half-an-hour after the attack started, we could find no trace of the attackers.

The following night, however, we were more successful as, acting on information we had previously received that after this Flying Column of the IRA had carried out an operation north of the Bandon River, they usually moved south and billetted in a group of farms in an area northeast of Kilbrittain, we took a strong party out in Crossley cars with a view to raiding these houses. The night was fairly moonlight and we therefore drove without lights. When about two miles from our destination we surprised a party of men trenching the road, who fled as we approached. Being unable to take the lorries further on account of the trench, we proceeded on foot, and on arrival at a cross road called Crushnalanniv close to our objective, we surprised an IRA picquet and accounted for four out of six of them, without any loss to ourselves. They were all armed with service rifles and carried about 50 rounds of SAA each. The firing, of course, alarmed the main body of the Flying Column who were billeted in the adjoining farms, and they immediately made off, but our tactics of surprise action, based on information available, had been entirely successful. The four dead men were subsequently identified as belonging to the local IRA Company which had evidently been called out for outpost duty during the night, while the main column rested.

A month or so later we were involved in what was probably one of the biggest fights in the open which took place during the 'Irish War', and this action is worth describing in some detail.

The man who, as I told you, was captured in the Upton train ambush turned out to be the Company Commander of the local IRA Company. This man, hoping to save his life, one day, asked to see the Brigade IO at Cork and informed him the headquarters of the 3rd Cork Brigade. The IRA were located in a group of farms in the Ballymurphy townland and there was a dug-out in the same locality, but he did not know exactly where. It was, therefore, arranged for a combined operation to be carried out at dawn the following morning by about 60 men from Bandon and a similar number from Cork, each party being allotted a definite group of farms and being responsible for having these surrounded at Zero hour. (6am). The Bandon party set out in lorries at 2.30am and motored to the Brinny Cross Roads, from which point the lorries were sent back to avoid disturbing the enemy. An escort of one officer and eight men were sent with the lorries; they had one LG and the drivers (eight in number) were also armed with revolvers. Orders were given to the officer to bring the lorries out again to meet the raiding party at Cross Barry at 7.30am and to proceed to this point by bounds with a patrol on foot out in front.

The raiding party then marched the remaining five miles and were in position at Zero. An exciting episode immediately took place as on entering one of the houses, the officer in charge of one patrol was fired at, at point blank range, by a man standing inside. The man then bolted out of the back door where he was shot dead by a sergeant who had been posted there. It is always well before entering the door to remain behind the door post till it is certain the way is clear. The dead man turned out to be the commandant of the 3rd Cork Brigade IRA.

Several other captures were effected in this neighbourhood, but at 7.30 am a heavy burst of firing was heard from Cross Barry and we at once guessed that our own lorry convoy with the skeleton escort had been ambushed there. We therefore quickly collected our party and moved down with a view to attacking the ambushers in the flanks and if possible, saving the lorries. We found the party of IRA which consisted of their Flying Column reinforced by local Companies about 100 strong in all – holding a position on the high ground overlooking the road and, as we approached, a series of explosions showed that they were beginning to blow up the lorries which had fallen into their hands. Following their usual tactics they then beat a hasty retreat, which was remarkable for the speed with which they moved across country and their main body succeeded in escaping before we could throw a cordon round them.

Our losses in this action (mostly among the lorry drivers and escort) were:, one officer and nine men killed and two officers and five men wounded, while we had two lorries completely destroyed. The losses of the IRA were four killed and three prisoners, and a number of wounded whom they succeeded in getting away. We also captured and destroyed their ammunition cart.

This was the last big ambush in that part of the country, and the moral effect of our sudden appearance on the enemy's flank made him very 'chary' of again laying ambushes on roads.

This was a very good example of the old saying that 'It is the unexpected that happens in war' – and especially in a war of this nature.

With regard to the trenching of the roads, we tried many expedients to neutralise this, but they were none of them very successful. We started by carrying light bridges on the lorries, which were for a time effective, but we found that, when the trenches became more than fourteen feet wide, the bridges would not take the weight of the lorry. The best method then is to 'ramp' the trench by sloping off the sides, but even that takes a long time. We also tried to fill them up with local civilian labour, but they would invariably be opened again within the next few days – probably by the same labour; in fact, the local inhabitants spent most of their time opening and filling in trenches during this period!

It is really impossible in warfare of this nature to keep road communications open if the enemy are determined to deny you the use of the roads.

This brought about an entirely new situation and in my next lecture, I will show you how we dealt with this situation.

LECTURE 2

Period April-July, 1921
In my last lecture I brought you up to the time when it became impossible any longer to use the roads for tactical purposes. It was obvious, therefore, that it was useless to rely any more on lorry movements, except for purposes of supply, etc. Summer was just coming on and it was decided to play the enemy at his own game, and form Military Mobile Columns, which would move on foot across country or by country lanes and thus avoid any danger of ambush. Further, by their power to move in any direction and at any time; these columns were able to make use of the element of surprise and also considerably lowered the enemy's morale by creating in him a feeling of insecurity.

Our columns consisted generally of two strong platoons, about two sections of which were mounted on cycles, and were accompanied by a cooker and a couple of GS limbered wagons to carry the men's kits. The men themselves were equipped as lightly as possible as we found mobility was of paramount importance to enable them to compete with the guerrilla tactics of the enemy.

Although we carried out a number of minor raids with these columns, and were constantly arresting some of the lesser lights of the IRA, we always insisted on regarding the enemy Flying Columns as our main objective as it was only by the destruction of those columns that we could hope to stop the IRA activities.

Our usual method of working these mobile columns was to

send out two or three at the same time and to allot each an area to work in, leaving empty an area, which we knew was a favourite resort of the IRA column. Then, during an agreed night all columns would move by a forced march, often of fifteen miles or so, and concentrate on the empty area and during the next day carry out a thorough search of this area.

With regard to what may be called the minor tactics of the mobile columns, we relied almost entirely on surprise action. If our objective was a village we would billet or bivouac five or six miles away, and then send off a bicycle patrol to make a sudden descent on the village at dusk. At other times, we would send out a patrol on foot to ambush a crossroads, for a portion of the night.

The principle we worked on was that, to obtain surprise, you must work well away from your transport, which on a still night can be heard miles off coming along the road. We almost invariably moved by night and rested by day, often doubling back on our foot-steps, so that the enemy never knew in which direction we were going to move next.

The result of these manoeuvres was that between April and July we were never once ambushed by the enemy.

In addition to the Mobile Columns a great deal of local patrolling was carried out by each Detachment, so as to keep the enemy on the move, and prevent him resting in any quiet area. The general idea was that there should be no quiet areas, and that the enemy columns should be constantly harassed.

The course usually pursued by the rebels during this period was to make off to the mountainous district to the northwest of our area when things became too hot for them. Several drives on a big scale in these mountains were organised by the Brigade, but generally speaking they had very little success. It was found to be almost impossible to keep secret the preparations necessary for controlling a large force in a small area and to feed them when they had got there.

It is, of course, a very difficult matter to round up a party of 20-30 Irregulars in this sort of warfare owing to their mobility and good intelligence, but we had conclusive evidence that, at the time of the Truce in July, our tactics of rapid movement and surprise had had such a demoralising effect on their nerves that in another few weeks the back of the Rebellion would have been broken.

The IRA during this period reverted to 'sniping' tactics. They regularly sniped policemen standing outside their Barracks, and on one occasion carried out simultaneous raids on all our Detachments, the object being to snipe the sentry and then make off. Fortunately they were only successful in one instance. An interesting incident occurred on the same day. One of their leaders was taking ammunition to a point of rendezvous for a raid on the Detachment at the Old Head of Kinsale, and was ambushed by a Mobile Column. His ammunition consisting of about 150 rounds of Mauser cartridges was captured though he himself escaped through having a scout on a horse 100 yards in front who gave the alarm in time.

It must be remembered that the IRA were no fools in the conduct of guerrilla warfare. Captured documents contained very clear and detailed instructions as to the best methods of carrying out different operations, and they even laid down certain principles of war – the majority of which were the same as ours. One of these principles was the principle of security, which was strictly observed by the rebel leader on this occasion, who saved himself by having a scout out in front.

Another step taken by the IRA during this period was the inauguration of a ruthless campaign against the Loyalists. Every success of ours was almost invariably followed by the murder or kidnapping of one or two Loyalists, who were, of course, entirely unprotected. Their object in doing this, when they saw they were being pressed in the active operations, was to induce the authorities to conclude a Truce. The culminating point in their policy of murder and arson was reached in June 1921, when Castle Bernard, the residence of Lord Bandon, was burnt to the ground and Lord Bandon himself was kidnapped. A few days later a well known lady, who had become an ardent Sinn Féin, came down to Castle Bernard and said to Lady Bandon, 'I have been sent down by our people to warn you that, unless the Government conclude a Truce, Lord Bandon will be killed.' The reply was – 'If that is all you have to say, you had better go home.'

In a struggle of this nature, the existence of a number of Loyalists among an otherwise hostile population is, and always will be, a powerful weapon in the hands of the rebels. Repeated demands will be received from these Loyalists for the protection of their persons and property, but this it will usually be impossible to grant. The only method of protecting them is to concentrate those who are willing to leave their homes in 'protected areas'. This it was proposed to do if the negotiations for a settlement had broken down. As long as they remain in the country they are a source of great weakness, as not only are they entirely at the mercy of the rebels, but they are also forced at the point of a revolver to keep the rebels supplied with funds and food.

Intelligence

I think it is clear from what I have already told you that it would have been impossible to carry out any operations without having a reasonably good Intelligence service. This was not fully realised in the early days of the struggle, and it was not till early in 1920 that the appointment of Battalion IOs was first made. The information in our possession at that time as to who was or who was not mixed up in the Sinn Féin movement was practically nil. What information there was was in the hands of the RIC and it took a lot of talking before you got very much out of them.

Objects of Intelligence
The objects of the Intelligence service were, I think, three in number:

(*i*) To obtain all possible information as to the organisation and plans of the IRA
(*ii*) To find out all about the inhabitants of the country.
(*iii*) To get a thorough knowledge of the topography of the country.

I will deal with these three objects in detail.

(*i*) *The Organisation and plans of the IRA*
It is obviously impossible to carry on a campaign unless you know who your opponents are. It was, therefore, necessary to study the organisation of the IRA and with this end in view an 'Order of Battle' of the IRA was issued from time to time from Brigade head-quarters and was kept up to date at Battalion headquarters. This order of battle included particulars as to the Battalion and Company organisation of the IRA Brigades, and the names of the officers in those units as far as known. It was, therefore, the duty of the Battalion IOs to find out who these officers were, where they lived and what they looked like.

With regard to the plans of the IRA it was very difficult to get any information about these in time to take action. This was on account of the very strict oath taken by members of the IRB who alone knew the details of any approaching operations. The ordinary members of the IRA were simply told to parade at a certain place at a certain time, and did not know the nature of the operations until they got there.

It therefore became necessary to study the personality and habits of the IRA leaders very carefully and after each operation carried out by them, to make deductions as to what the next step was likely to be. It was by the use of this method that we obtained our success in the Crushnalanniv patrol encounter as explained to you in my first lecture.

(ii) The Inhabitants of the Country

The attitude adopted by the Crown Forces towards the ordinary inhabitants of the country varied very much in different localities. In some places the attitude taken up was that the whole population was hostile, and should be treated accordingly. This was often the attitude adopted by the Auxiliaries. Personally, I was convinced that such an attitude was fundamentally wrong, and that in conditions of this nature, you must at all costs distinguish the sheep from the wolves. If you fail to do so, you drive the whole population into the hands of the enemy.

This again is one of the duties of the Battalion IO. He must find out all he can about the political sympathies of every civilian: if hostile, whether they are extremists or not; if friendly, whether they are prepared to give information and, if so, what their information is worth.

I found the best way to do this was to keep a large scale six inch map on the wall of my office. On the maps every farm and detached house is marked, and as we got the information, I filled in the name of the occupier of each farm or house. I also kept in a book a note of the political sympathies of these occupiers. I was, therefore, able before any officer went out on a raid, to give him all available information as to whom he was likely to find in each house.

(iii) Topography of the Country

Under this heading comes information as to the most covered approach to each farm or house: the existence of any lanes or 'borheens' down which any of the enemy might escape and which should be 'blocked' before the house was approached; good view points from which observation could be kept on the surrounding country during operations; and the state of roads, tracks, etc.

1. *Methods of Obtaining Information*

Owing to the secret nature of the hostile forces and the strict oath taken by then, bribes were of little use, and, although a limited amount of money was available for this purpose, I only on one occasion found any opportunity of using it. The most profitable methods were as follows:

> (*i*) Most important of all, an IO must move about the country and hunt for information. It will not come to him if he sits in his office all day.
>
> (*ii*) He must keep in close touch with the Loyalists – especially those who are not afraid to tell him what they know.

This is not always an easy thing to do, as if the IRA suspected a Loyalist of giving information or being too friendly with the Crown Forces, it meant certain death to him. It was our usual practice therefore to approach their houses after dark, and very long night journeys often had to be made in order to do this.

Captured documents were often of great value. Notebooks often contained the rolls of the local Company, list of arms and ammunition in possession, etc. The well known Lord Mayor of Cork, Terence MacSwiney, was captured as the result of a letter ordering a litigant to appear at a Sinn Féin Court which fell into our hands.

Information obtained direct from members of the IRA. This was very rare, but I had in my area an officer of one of the local Companies whom I had had convicted of some small offence and sentenced to six months imprisonment. As he was the owner of a farm, he found it very inconvenient to go to prison, and so suggested that, if I would get his sentence postponed, he would give me weekly reports of the state of his Company. This I agreed to, but threatened to enforce the sentence if the reports did not come in regularly. He proved very useful.

Anonymous letters. These were very numerous and had to be treated with a good deal of suspicion. It was often the case of one family trying to get a bit of its own back on a neighbouring family.

2. *Functions of the Battalion Intelligence Officers*
The main duties of the Battalion IO in warfare of this nature are, I think the following:

(*i*) To obtain Intelligence of the nature I have indicated above.
(*ii*) To submit to his CO plans for suggested operations based on the nature of intelligence in his possession.
(*iii*) Identify prisoners when captured. This was one of the most difficult things in the whole campaign. The hostile leaders were seldom known by sight and they invariably gave false names. A number of them thus slipped through our hands after being actually captured.

Picture 50 to 60 civilians lined up in front of you, out of which you have to pick any of the IRA leaders. At first it seems almost impossible, but after a little practice one becomes able to select a few likely 'types'. It then becomes a question of getting these few men identified and here the IOs' knowledge of the local civilians comes in.

A successful method which I practised for some time was to ask any of the old inhabitants for the names of the suspected men. If the names they gave did not agree with those given themselves, you knew you had got a 'wrong un'.

Of course, we could not keep a man indefinitely if we could not identify him, and we frequently had to release men whom we were convinced were rebel leaders, from sheer inability to find out who they were.

I think it will be clear from what I have said that the duties of the Battalion IO are very important ones: in fact, the whole success of the conduct of operations in any given area really depends on him. I am of the opinion, therefore, that this position should be filled by a fairly senior officer, who has sufficient standing in the Battalion to enable him to carry out the duties I have described.

That the Intelligence officers did not escape the attention of the IRA is shown by the followings instructions, dated the 16th February, 1921 – 'it has been decided by the IRA headquarters to compile a list of "aggressive" Intelligence Officers as soon as possible. In determining what IOs would come under the heading of "aggressive", the following points would be a deciding factor in any decision arrived at:

> 'Do they accompany the Military in raids?
> Were they concerned in the arrest of Volunteers?
> Were they concerned in giving evidence against Volunteers?
> Were they concerned in the death of any Volunteers?
> Were they concerned in having to go "on the run?"
> Do they spy on Volunteers or Volunteers' Houses?
> Do they take part in reprisals?
> You will also give their full names and addresses with a footnote showing what you think they are worth.'

It would be very interesting to see what sort of a report one got!

3. Training of the Troops

A guerrilla war of this nature demands a very high state of training on the part of troops. The majority of the operations are carried out in small parties and a great many of them at night. Individuality in the NCO and Private Soldier is, therefore, of great value. In this regard the whole Army was seriously handicapped in 1920-21, as a very large proportion of the men in the ranks were youngsters of two or three years' service, or even less. The work from the Private Soldier's point of view was very arduous, as escorts were constantly being called for. In addition, it was necessary to put restrictions on the area in which the soldiers could 'walk out', for fear of their being kidnapped.

A large number of the raids and searches carried out were naturally unsuccessful, and in these conditions, there was great danger of the troops becoming tired and slack. To avoid this, we decided to try and make them interested in the proceedings which we did by means of lectures and talks on local IRA celebrities, etc. We also encouraged them to bring in any information they might pick up. The result was extremely good, as the troops, almost without exception, became very keen on the work and took a great interest in everything that was done.

Of course, the work there was excellent training for young troops, as they always had to be very much on the alert to prevent being surprised – especially when they were on sentry duty.

Their chief failing was in the lack of Musketry training they had received. In this type of warfare targets are few and fleeting. I think those who have tried it will agree that it is no easy matter to hit a single man running fast and across country, especially when you have often run some distance yourself. Troops taking part in such warfare should have very thorough musketry training as each individual man really becomes a sniper.

4.Use of Arms other than Infantry
Artillery
Permission was not given for the use of Artillery till the summer of 1922, at Belleck, and therefore we had no experience of it. I do

not consider, however, that there is any scope for the use of artillery in warfare of this nature, unless the rebels form themselves into larger bodies than they did in Ireland. As it was, there were really no targets upon which artillery could fire.

Tanks

These were too slow moving and too noisy to be of much use in the very open warfare of the South of Ireland. They might, perhaps, be useful in large cities for clearing streets, or taking on rebel strongholds, such as the Four Courts in Dublin.

Armoured Cars

Two types of armoured car were used – the heavy and slow Peerless, and the fast Rolls Royce. Both were very useful.

(*i*) The Peerless. This was used chiefly to economise manpower in escorts, etc. It was suitable to accompany three-ton lorry convoys, and also for local work, e.g., mail escort to the station, escort for officers drawing pay, ration parties, etc. It was a mistake to send Crossley cars with the Peerless AC, as the reduced speed of the latter caused a heavy strain on the axles of the Crossleys.

(ii) The Rolls Royce. The chief uses of this were:

(*a*) To escort Crossley cars or Sunbeam touring cars. In this way they were usually employed when Brigade commanders or staff officers wanted to make a tour of the Brigade area.

(*b*) For offensive operations. They were used with great success for sudden descents on given areas in towns, or on outlying country villages, when the state of the road permitted. Owing to their speed and quiet running they were particularly suitable for this work. They carried a crew of four and were armed with a Vickers Gun. A Hotchkiss gun was often carried also, as a reserve and for use if the AC broke down.

Aeroplanes

Owing to the shortage of landing grounds these were little used. It is doubtful whether an airman can see much in a country of this nature, but he should, I think, be able to reconnoitre roads and report whether they are trenched or blocked. Also if an ambush is reported in a definite locality the RAF could be asked to make a reconnaissance of that locality. This I did on one occasion, sending the request by wireless, and having a message with the report dropped in our Barrack Square at Kinsale about a couple of hours later. Where landing grounds were available, aeroplanes would be of great assistance as a quick means of transport for Commanders and Staff Officers.

5. *Staff Duties*

The Brigades in the South had very large areas to control, and their duties, especially after the declaration of Martial Law, became very arduous.

The Cork Brigade at one time had as many as nine Battalions besides a large amount of MT etc. The question, which then arose was whether it was better to maintain the existing Brigade and increase the staff, or form a new Brigade and divide the area. The former alternative was adopted, the argument in favour of it being that it would take a new Brigade staff some weeks or even months to pick up the threads of a vary intricate situation. The existing Brigade staff was, therefore, increased until it consisted of:

1 BM
1 Assistant BM
3 Staff Captains (one of whom dealt entirely with legal mat
ters)
2 Intelligence Officers
1 Signal Officer
1 MT Officer.

Even then the work was found to be too much for one staff and after the Truce, the area was actually divided into two in view of possible further trouble. The duties of the 'G' Staff are to co-ordinate the work of other units, to arrange for the maintenance of communications between units, and Brigade HQ, and to disseminate information. The majority of the actual operations must be left to the initiative of the unit commanders, but the work of the Mobile Columns should be contained by Brigade headquarters.

6. *General*

Ruses – All ranks must always be on the alert to avoid being taken in by the enemy ruses. Reports were frequently received of the IRA ambushes in outlying districts, these reports having been spread by the IRA themselves with a view to inducing us to send out a party to clear the road. This party would then be attacked on the way out.

The people who wage guerrilla warfare are usually adepts in the art of 'bluff'. On one occasion, the secretary of the Demobilized Soldiers and Sailors Federation asked for an interview with me. On being admitted he offered to help us. We had several interviews until I discovered one day that he also held the position of Battalion commandant in the IRA and that his visits were designed to gain first-hand information of the interior of our Barracks!

Ruses were also employed on our side quite frequently. One of the most successful was what was known as the 'Q' lorry. This was an ordinary three-ton lorry, armour plated inside and loaded with a number of blankets. Inside was a crew with a couple of MGs. The idea was to send this lorry out into a desolate part of the country, where it would break down and be ostensibly left on the side of the road. The enemy would then come along to burn it, which gave the occupants the opportunity of some very good shooting.

Routine Movements. These were sometimes necessary, but

should be, wherever possible, avoided. The Macroom Ambush of Auxiliaries and a great many other successful IRA operations were made possible by quite unnecessary routine movements. When routine movements are unavoidable, those making them should be accompanied by an escort capable of dealing with any situation that may arise.

The enemy, in a struggle of this nature, disregards all the ordinary rules of war. It is the duty of all ranks, therefore, to avoid any risk of being kidnapped. A good rule is to always ask yourself, before proceeding anywhere either on business or pleasure, 'can the enemy possibly expect that I should make this journey?' If there is any chance of him doing so, then adequate precautions should be taken.

Every civilian should be looked upon as a potential enemy. It was clearly laid down in instructions issued that the safety of the soldiers is the first consideration. A favourite trick of the IRA was to mix with the crowd in a busy thoroughfare and suddenly make an assault on any military or police patrol that might be passing.

7. Suggested Future Tactics

As far as I know, no official book has been published on the subject of guerrilla warfare, such as we had in Ireland, but I will give my own ideas on the best tactics to be pursued should such conditions recur.

The question appears to resolve itself into the rival claims of the Block-House system, such as was adopted in South Africa, and the Mobile Column system.

The possibility of building block-houses was often discussed in 1921, but we reckoned then that to work any block-house system, we should require a great many more troops than there were at the time in the whole of Ireland. The country is so thick and intricate that it would be impossible to stop small parties of men getting through unless the block-houses were very close together.

On the other hand, if sufficient men were available, a line of temporary post or 'stops' along the edge of the area being worked by the Mobile Column, would, I think, be of great assistance, as they would restrict the area of manoeuvres at the disposal of the enemy. In our area, for example, these might have been placed along the lines of the Bandon River while the mobile columns were working to the south of it.

In either case, whether block-houses are established or not, offensive action must be taken and this can be best done with a number of mobile columns moving about the country and mutually co-operating with each other. The composition of a column of this sort, of course, depends on the strength of the opposition likely to be encountered, but the basis in which it should be worked out is as follows:

Required:
A. Infantry
(*i*) Escort for horse transport
(*ii*) A bicycle patrol for long distance action
(*iii*) A foot patrol for short distance action

B. Cavalry or MTs: A small body to work in conjunction with the Infantry.

Their role would be to ride on ahead by lanes or country tracks and occupy a position from which they could observe anybody trying to escape from the Infantry. They would then be in a position to ride them down and capture them.

A number of mounted gunners had arrived in Ireland at the time of the Truce, and this was the way in which it was intended to employ them.

On the above lines, a suitable organisation for a mobile Column during the Operations under review would have been:

Infantry: two strong platoons – say 60 OR of which two section would be mounted on bicycles.

MI: One Troop.

Each of these columns should be supplied with some form of WT, to enable them to be controlled from a central position. This was a deficiency from which we suffered considerably in 1921, as we found that very often the best information was obtained by Brigade headquarters in Cork and they had no means of transmitting it quickly to the column in the field.

Another difficulty, which handicapped us severely, was the system by which the meat and bread rations for the Mobile Columns had to be obtained from the local towns. This meant that the butcher and baker in these towns had to be warned a day or so beforehand to have these rations ready, which was practically equivalent to publishing the directions of our next move. The element of surprise was practically forfeited. It is important that the Columns employed on work of this nature should be as self contained as far as their supplies are concerned. They should either carry them with them in the form of preserved rations or be accompanied by a butcher and purchase directly from the farms.

It is interesting to note that Sir John Moore, when he was stationed at Bandon in 1798, was confronted with a very similar problem to that which faced us in 1920-21 and that he also adopted the Mobile Column system, working it in much the same way as we did in 1921, ie, several columns co-operating and all working towards one given point.

Conclusion

The importance of the strict observance of the Principles of War as laid down in FSR is perhaps more clearly seen in this type of warfare than in any other:

(i) Every operation or small raid must have an objective
(ii) Offensive action is essential to success
(iii) Surprise must be aimed at in every operation, closely allied to this is Security, ie, safety from surprise
(iv) The Crown Forces had to be concentrated before offensive action could be taken. It was only thus that Economy of Force could be effected and the required number of troops made available for active operations
(v) Mobile Columns are useless unless they have real mobility, and finally
(vi) Close co-operation between neighbouring area commanders is essential. Otherwise quiet districts will be left into which the enemy can retire and rest when heavily pressed.

CHAPTER 9

Field Marshal Bernard Law Montgomery

Details

This letter is part of a collection of personal papers of Montgomery's stored in the Imperial War Museum. Montgomery's military career began as a second lieutenant in the Royal Warwickshire Regiment in 1908; he was promoted Lieutenant in 1910, and Captain in 1914. He served as a Brigade Major in France from 1915 to 1917, as a General Staff Officer, Grade 2 (Temporary Major) from 1917 to 1918, and as a General Staff Officer, Grade 1 (Temporary Lieutenant Colonel) from 1918 to 1919. During 1919, he served with the British Army of the Rhine for several months, as a General Staff Officer, Grade 2. He returned to the role of Brigade Major with the 17th Infantry Brigade in Cork, from 5 January 1921 to 23 May 1922. Montgomery left Ireland to serve in the United Kingdom, in the Southern and later the Northern Commands. He served at the Staff College, Camberley, from 1926 to 1929, as a Deputy Assistant Adjutant General, and was an Instructor at the Indian Army Staff College at Quetta from 1934 to 1937. Montgomery returned to England as a Brigade Commander with Southern Command. In 1938, he was appointed a Major General,

A shop in Washington Street, Cork, is destroyed by explosives as part of an official reprisal.

A house is reduced to ruins in Meelin, County Cork, as part of an official reprisal, 20 January 1921.

Soldiers searching civilians in Meelin, County Cork, 1921.

and given command of a division in Palestine and Transjordan. He commanded the Third Division in France in 1939, and in 1942 he was given command of the Eighth Army, winning the Battle of El Alamein. He was the Allied assault leader at Normandy. Later he was given command of the Twenty-First Army Group and promoted to Field Marshal. Montgomery was Commander in Chief of the British Army of Occupation in Germany. In 1946, he was made Chief of the Imperial General Staff. From 1951 to 1958 he was Deputy Supreme Allied Commander in Europe. He retired from military service in 1958.

A LETTER WRITTEN to Lt General A.C. Percival and dated York 14/10/23.

My Dear Percival,
I give below a few notes on the points you asked about.

Staff Duties
These became somewhat arduous owing to the large area a Brigade to look after, and the number of units it had to deal with. In the 17th Brigade, we had at one time nine battalions, and the work was frightfully hard. There were two alternatives in order to ease this.

(*a*) Create more Brigades
(*b*) Keep the same number of Brigades, but increase the staff of each.

Alternative (*b*) was adopted at first, as it was considered that the situation was so complex that a new Brigadier would take several months to pick up the threads, this of course was quite true. So they increased our staff and I had three staff captains, in addition to a large 'I' staff. But it was really too much, and after the

British troops in Meelin, County Cork, during an official reprisal, 1921.

'Truce' had been on some time and it looked as if the show would break out again they split up the areas, and created fresh brigades.

I am certain that the best procedure was mobile columns mutually co-operating with each other. But they must have WT, so that they can be operated direct from Brigade headquarters if required, we often found that the best intelligence was received by us in Cork, and if columns had no WT we could not take advantage of it.

Attitude of Staff towards Civilians
We were not brought into such close touch with the Loyalists as you were, and the result was I think that we did not appreciate their suffering to the same extent. Personally, my whole attention was given to defeating the rebels and it never bothered me a bit how many houses were burnt. I think I regarded all civilians as 'Shinners', and I never had any dealings with any of them.

Aeroplanes
These were really of no use to use, except as a quick and safe means of getting from one place to another.

Even then the landing grounds were few and far between. The pilots and observers knew nothing whatever about the war, on the conditions under which it was being fought, and were not therefore in a position to be able to help much.

General Remarks
My own view is that to win a war of this sort you must be ruthless. Oliver Cromwell, or the Germans, would have settled it in a very short time. Nowadays public opinion precludes such methods, the nation would never allow it, and the politicians would lose their jobs if they sanctioned it. That being so I consider that Lloyd-George was really right in what he did, if we had gone on we could probably have squashed the rebellion as a temporary measure, but

it would have broken out again like an ulcer the moment we removed the troops. I think the rebels would probably refused battles, and hidden away their arms etc. until we had gone. The only way therefore was to give them some form of self government, and let them squash the rebellion themselves, they are the only people who could really stamp it out, and they are still trying to do so and as far as one can tell they seem to be having a fair amount of success. I am not however in close touch with the situation over there, but it seems to me that they have had more success than we had. I arrived at the above conclusion after a great deal of thought on the subject. You probably will not agree.

Yours ever,
B.L. Montgomery.

CHAPTER 10

Lieutenant Colonel Evelyn Lindsay Young

Details

This is from an account held in the private papers of Lt Col Lindsay Young in the Liddell Hart Centre for Military Archives in King's College London. Lindsay Young was educated at Trinity College Dublin, and began his military career in the Dublin University Officer Training Corps. He was commissioned into the Regular Army in 1913. He was a temporary Lieutenant with the 8th Battalion Gordon Highlanders from 1914 to 1915. He was promoted to Lieutenant in 1915, and served with the 1st and 2nd Battalions, the 19th Punjabi Regiment, Indian Army from 1915 to 1920. He saw action in the Mahsud rising of 1917, in the Marris rising of 1918, and in the 3rd Afghan War on the North West Frontier in 1919. He was an acting Lieutenant Colonel in the Indian Army in 1920, before transferring to the Connaught Rangers. He served in Ireland from 1920 to 1922. On the disbandment of the Connaught Rangers, he transferred to the Leicestershire Regiment in 1922. He served in the Sudan in 1924 during the mutiny of Egyptian troops. Lindsay Young again served in India from 1932 to 1941, and saw action in Waziristan on the North West Frontier in 1939. He was the commanding officer of 1st Battalion Leicestershire Regiment from 1939

153

to 1942. During the Second World War, he served in Malaya and from 1944 with the British Army in north west Europe. He retired from the Army in 1947.

Under the Shadow of Darkness – Ireland, 1920

I STEPPED DOWN from the gangplank, gave Davy Roberts a half-crown, accepted a daily paper in return; and 'Davy' gave me his smile and 'th' top o' the morning' instead of the change. Davy beamed upon me – my return to Ireland was propitious.

Half and hour afterwards I was at Broadstone, where I ate a breakfast of smutty eggs and bacon and missed the train. On sauntering into the city the old streets seemed just the same, the wreak of the 'rebellion' had left little mark; Sackville Street a little batted, Trinity still flourishing, Grafton Street not quite so gay – the 'Grafton Street Brigade' did not seem so active, thinned off by the war perhaps. The need of fodder set me wandering off for an early lunch at my old grazing ground the Dolphin: even here the same old spirit prevailed, and – joyful moment – some of the old hands recognised me; old Billy was there, hair as white as ever, but doing still slower motion studies than ever before – to cross the spacious floor was quite a route march for his old legs; but he gave me a fine lunch of his own choice, beef – fresh Kildare beef- and butter galore ... this way back in '20; and old Billy assured me that they'd had Kildare beef during the whole war. It was almost worth returning to Ireland to be shot at if one could fill one's belly with this fettle instead of the anaemic fare of Angleterre.

Two hours later I was been whisked westward in the western mail. As we reached Mullingar some fat priests boarded the train; 'Don't look at them for pity's sake!' said the nervous subaltern's wife in the carriage, 'they may shoot you' – such is war! Soon as we arrived at our destination and slipping my traps on a car, I missed the lorry which had come for me and drove up the three miles of road to the old barracks on the bay which was to be my home for a year or more. Days rolled on peacefully. Soon one began to believe that there could be no such thing as a hidden gun or gunmen. Life was glorious in that late September and the mackerel fishing in the bay was a quick death exhibition; boating on the river or a sail or motorboat expedition on the lakes revived old memories of the joy of life in Ireland. But one dirty night the paradise on earth was swept way. Just when the midnight mail was rushed by, as I lay in bed, I heard the Poop! Poop! Poop! of shots in the town. Soon the barracks were astir, down went the troops to the town in the only lorry followed by the old tank spitting fire into the midnight air like a dragon.

An RIC driver had been shot – but the penalty was to be paid. Somehow or other Britishers seem to let sleeping dogs lie till they want them! The information seemed good then for the intelligence service had not been started. Cork gun-men and others, priding themselves on concealment, were dragged from their beds; and their end was not less swift than that of the policemen. An eye for an eye! and half a dozen of yours lucky enough – that was the word for that night ... but the station door bears the bullet marks still, and perhaps there's one lad in Ireland who is still grateful to one who found him wounded and left him for 'dead'.

Coroners inquests had ceased to be in Ireland so the night's work was brought to a military inquiry instead. It was difficult to get witnesses as they were either intimidated or mysteriously disappeared. The court carried on with a fine audience filled with spies; and a general creepy feeling throughout the proceeding that the court itself might at any instant become the subject of another enquiry into shooting. Little evidence was adduced as to the killing of the RIC driver. The junior members asked somewhat pointed questions feeling somewhat hot about the matter it was even adduced that the victim had not been hit in a necessarily vital spot, but had succumbed on reaching the hospital – half a mile away – to which he had been sent by a doctor without the bleeding even having been arrested. Curiously enough the same medico left the country very quickly having been embarked for the east as a ship's surgeon. Fate, perhaps retribution, acted curiously and rapidly – the self same doctor when he had been at sea but three weeks, died of a tropical disease.

The civilian hotheads decided to hold another court of enquiry on their own, and with this object sent registered letters to the Chief of the RIC demanding his attendance. The 'court' was suppressed. Constantly starved for news the local Yellow Express found in the recent happenings a fountain of copy – gorged with the unexpected feast and exasperated by the suppression of the local civilians' 'enquiry', the editor's pen crossed into the paths of indiscretion ... 'the dead policeman was a public danger – the young men had only rushed to disarm him – it was the duty of everyone there, if he could, to shoot him as he would a mad dog' ... 'the military court had unscrupulously endeavoured to twist the enquiry in one direction for the sake of saving the "police" and the English government' ... 'the chief of the RIC was branded as a public liar'.... 'the police were sweating with panic'... and so on. Finally the editor finished with a polite remark regarding the spies 'as pimps in petticoats' and informed his readers that there would be more in the next edition. Unfortunately for him, there was no next edition – for the next morning the street outside the Yellow Express office was a mass of coloured papers, inside the printing and linotype machines were wreaked, the safe 'cracked' and all was a shambles.

For some weeks the military and police had been congratulating themselves on the comparative peace which had reigned since the Yellow Express had succumbed. In the mess, after dinner, we were just settling in for a quiet evening when in rushed the intelligence officer brandishing some large printed sheets.

Lindsay-Young describes the use of a tank in Mullingar, County Westmeath. However, no picture of this type of operation survives. The above shows a similar type of patrol in a French street during the First World War.

'It's started again, Sir: The Yellow Express,' he said to the general. That superior officer seized a copy and the others present crowded around the remaining copies. Everyone looked tense and serious. Yes! It was the real thing. The same heading in Gaelic characters. On the bottom was a large inscription, also in Gaelic, which one versed in Irish translated as 'God save Ireland'.

Expressions of disgust, annoyance, wonder were evoked as the paper was read. If the Yellow Express had been hot before – this time it was white hot ... A long harangue from the editor – news of 'Another victory for Ireland' – a description of 'A night of horror in "c" accompanied by Revolting Scenes of Slaughter, Sacrilege, and Systematic Sabotage' – 'Military assist RIC in Assassination, Looting and Arson' – Thus ran the headings. The body of this edition was hotter still. Citizens were called upon to 'hurl back into the raging sea of nations the tattered mangled remnants of savagery which, in the shape of England, sought to retain their octupean grip' ... to gird themselves around the loins, and keep ever watching ever waiting, for the SIGNAL, then! set about the work prepared for them and shake off the loathsome pestilence rotting the flesh from off their frames ... the chief of the RIC (not now ignominiously branded as a public liar) was described as follows:

He who has won for himself position, power and preposterous pay, by betraying his country and his religion to the Sassenach! He who sits at home and shuffles his pack whilst his green coated minions go out and commit the atrocities which he has planned! Who has surrounded himself with heartless adulterers and bloodthirsty assassins, and has appointed them officers of the law.

The General turned an inquiring eye on the Intelligence Officer. 'Do the police know of this?' he asked.

'They captured several copies in the mail last night, Sir.'

'Come to my room X!' said our superior officer, leading the way and looking very serious.

Now as it happened that the chief of the RIC was very pleased with his own capabilities and his own importance – so much so that he was somewhat blasphemously known amongst the troops as 'Creeping Jesus' or 'Crawling Christ'! Therefore on reading the pungent statements about himself he took the paper as being a personal assault upon his exalted position, and his desire to capture the Yellow Express was insuperable. He decided to take action. And to take it without the knowledge of the troops, thus gaining a coup on his own, and avenging his adversary. Soon the wires hummed. Out went the police cars to make a lengthy search in likely places. The rank and file were filled with ardour to capture the horrible Yellow Press. The police scoured the country for several days without effect. The military took no action.

A few days later an irate police officer appeared in barracks, and made valiant efforts to get 'disciplinary action' taken against two officers. He had not, however, warned the military of his intended action – and thus could not be warned in return. The latest and fiery edition of the Yellow Press had been printed in barracks by the two officers into whose hands the title plates had fallen.

The military organisation grew, transport expanded, brass-hats increased, our little barracks was invaded; a brigade was born, with an intelligence service – marvellous and efficient in its own opinion, so Christmas drew nigh. While the fodder was good; and the funds lasted; we believed in filling the men with it – there must be many an outcast soldier, Irish or Sassenach, who remembers in his hunger a good Xmas dinner – poor fellows! What a lot has been done for them?

We had a fine dinner arranged for our lads: pigs and almost a bird for every two men; with a special fellow toiled off to fatten them up. He took a great interest in his new profession as a bird fattener and had a name for almost every bird. One day, talking to him, I asked him the name of his largest bird, which was so fat and big and regal that his knees seemed to bend together under him; 'Thart one Sor,' he replied, 'Him's King Garge.' Just before the feast, a couple of destroyers came beating up the bay and settled down at the anchorage. Soon we had the welcome company of some of the Sister Service in our mess. The Navy were in trouble. Soon the be-whiskered commander broached his innermost secrets to us – he could get no birds for the Navy's Christmas dinner. Quickly we put his troubles to rest. 'Stay to dinner with us and we'll fix you up.' The meal finished the guests were led away to dress their part. Decked in mufti with muffler and face blackened even the most senior member of the Senior Service was unrecognisable. Bungled into cars, off sped the party into the blackness of the night to a suitable distance where sins were untraceable and the forfeit taken would in some way balance taxes unpaid.

Many a barn and yard gave up its best. All worked with willing hands. With feathers flying and necks wringing midst the chuckling of the victors the murder and carnage ensured. At last the task was completed. The sacrificial cars sped homeward with their feathered offerings. The victors blood stained, feather covered but victorious. The Navy must have had a good feed; but the cleaning of the general's car, which had been borrowed, was a job!

Christmas passed joyfully – so we filled in the long winter nights sometimes regaling ourselves; with the kind permission of the brigadier; with selections played on a captured band, sometimes acting scenes of rebel heroes for the amusement of ourselves and at the expense, sometimes of our guests. At other times our quietness was interrupted by a call to arms; sometimes the mails had to be raided – a tedious job as a whole night's entertainment, but many interested pieces of information were gathered. The amount of money which went through the post was surprising, almost more surprising than the things which people write to each other ... a man perhaps telling his lover that his wife's attractions had waned; another telling, indiscreetly, the contents of his dreams; another – a poem of a dead Sinn Féiner, written by a girl ... an admirer! perhaps a lover!

The collection of intelligence was one of the most interesting and risky games over there. Our intelligence was not too intelligent and methods employed were sometimes unorthodox; the only rule for this work was 'get the information' – the means of procuring it were left to the individual.

Local intelligence in some cases became a failure because intelligence officers often adopted the same method of adducing information from a captured farm-hand as that employed to interrogate a man of even better education than the interrogator himself, and there was a total ignorance of the true temperament of the people. Once an IO finding a man on the road had reported himself during a round up, as a CDB man (Congested Districts Board) arrested him and handed him over thinking he was an illicit diamond buyer (IDB) as the person who carried out the arrest was a Jew it was easy to follow the path of association which his brain followed. It was ludicrous to watch an interrogator trying to badger information out of a doctor, or other professional man by means of a two foot ruler and gun; or hanging on the throat of a crofter, whose only tongue was Gaelic, tying to make him give information in English.

Information given or volunteered by a friend was best ignored – if only for the safety of one's friend – the source of information might leek out or be adduced by a too astute enemy. There was one sad example of this worth repeating. A loyalist wrote in giving information and by some means or other the letter was obtained for period by the enemy. In order to get a sample of the writer's handwriting to trace the author, he was approached while playing golf by a man with a slate who appeared to be deaf and dumb. By means of the slate the 'dumb man' induces the victim to write down certain questions.

These were taken away and thus the writer was traced and killed. It so happened that the 'dumb man' was also traced, or believed to be, and a certain priest was induced to leave his house one night on a visit to the sick. Some weeks later children playing in a part of the country found the partially covered body of the selfsame priest near a bog.

On occasions the 'third degree' was employed to extract information, sometimes with amusing results, at others causing the total breakdown of the captive with an accompanying flow of information and tears. One place chosen for this process was an old water mill. A couple of prisoners were led into the outer room of the mill – one being a fake prisoner. The 'fake' was taken into the inner room through the floor of which water rushed; a violent interrogation then ensued during which the 'fake' made constant refusals to give information. Finally there was a clanking of chains; the grinding of machinery ... a dull thud ... a shriek! ... a splash!!! The interview had ended.

With a horse laugh back came the inquisitors for their 'next' victim; usually he would become tractable on seeing the black rushing water below or on being reminded of it by an application of cold water.

One night, the victim happened to be older than usual and perhaps the shabbiness of his clothes prevented the captors from perceiving that he was a man of some intelligence. The inquisitors watch eagerly for the expected signs of fear as the whole play was acted for his benefit. In the inner room the explanation of his impending fate was given; but the prisoner, instead of becoming overcome with the usual cold fear, drew himself up and looking round scornfully on his captors calmly said – 'Drown me in that? There isn't a foot of water in that race – I happen to be the engineer who built this mill!'

Sometimes, in the case of a killing, information was adduced from prisoners believed to be connected with the event by actually re-acting the killing before them – a most trying ordeal. A room was curtained in two, on one side the prisoner was seated and left sitting for some duration in the uncanny silent darkness; perhaps after a time a cold wet clammy hand would silently embrace him or wander over his face in the gloom ...then suddenly the curtain would drop! and behold before him lay the cold waxen face of the victim in it's funeral shroud; the very wounds being accurately depicted. Few who had actually had to do with the deed could resist such an appeal.

Several times I was detailed to take despatches to GHQ in Dublin. It's not such a very nice job to arrive in North City at midnight in the winter, and to have to make one's way on foot from Broadstone to Parkgate when there's shooting about. I looked as rough as possible in mufti with hat pulled down over the eyes as, with the dispatches fixed to the inner part of my leg, I trudged onwards. I lost my way and had to adopt the somewhat risky procedure of asking the way to the nearest landmark – the quays – from which point direction I knew the way ... on a night like this every lonely individual in the streets might have been a mobile arsenal ... or possible each had a dozen notches in his gun – you know the feeling! I decided that the oldest person one met would be the more likely to be less implicated in the struggle for the birth of the new nation. To doubly secure my position I addressed him in the little Irish I knew, but he explained that he knew no Irish – few people in Dublin do. So I gained the information from him using my best imitation of a Dublin North Circular Road accent – it was effective, and I passed on in safety. Parkgate was reached without further mishap; entry seemed surprisingly easy, for I passed the guard without being challenged and climbed up the dusty stairs to the duty-room to report. I entered the room unannounced – the tired looking officer, on my entry, made a furtive grab at his pistol: then withdrew his hand leaving the weapon on the table with the butt pointing politely towards me. I received a receipt for my packet and lingered a little somewhat amused. 'I'd like to say' said I 'that although I admire your second line of defence, I passed your guard on the gate and came up here unchallenged.' 'Good God!' cried the tired one 'impossible'. He seized the telephone, almost terrified at the thought that he might possibly have been assassinated, and proceeded to make exhaustive enquiries. The guard turned out and all below seemed in uproar in the yard. I am rather sorry I had told him – I had some difficulty in getting out.

Much of the 'work' in our part of the country seemed to be carried out at night. The main difficulty was the procuring of the necessary transport. Once a car was procured from a doctor who unfortunately discovered its location and put the matter in the hands of his solicitor demanding hire and compensation. The matter rapidly developed into an acute duel which necessitated the owner being constantly ushered away from the precincts of the local headquarters. At last one wag hit upon the brilliant idea of turning the medico's political opinions upon him. Some notepaper had been captured from the enemy bearing the Sinn Féin badge and flag in colours. The doctor in question shortly received a letter purporting to come from the IRA headquarters; it stated that it had come to the notice of the 'authorities' that he had been corresponding with the enemy and trading with them regarding the hire of his car, in consequence of which, if dealings continued his loyalty to the cause would be questioned and a personal example would be made of him. The car remained 'free of hire' for some months.

There was in one district a man who always assumed a very supercilious air. He wore a pointed beard, which beard, in spite of its wearer's undoubted loyalty to the 'cause' and the fact that his son was 'on the run', was said by those who did not like him to make him like King George in appearance. The offence he had received by this likeness he would tell his friends of with a very annoyed air, at the same time leaving little doubt that he felt some pride in his resemblance to Royalty. One cold January night he was visited, his house ransacked, and the missing son searched for. However one side of the 'King George's beard' was removed by a few rapid strokes, and the Royal prototype's decadent chin exposed.

News came from the district that the owner of the 'Royal Beard' had been confined to the house for several days while a razor was procured from the town. Finally he appeared somewhat shame-facedly in public with a 'minus 4' chin and excused himself by stating that he had perforce to remove the royal emblem owing to an attack of eczema.

The staff themselves sometimes came in for a little chipping. Once the brigadier was at first somewhat surprised to hear from a certain CO, who he was visiting at a distance, that he did not want any more visits from a certain intelligence officer who had a peculiar command of the English language, because that officer always required a lot of labour after he had gone. 'Does he want a lot of work done, or what?' inquired the brigadier. 'Well' said the CO, 'I always have to employ large fatigue parties when he has gone – to sweep up all the H's he always drops.'

On another occasion the GOC was going through a circular with a unit regarding indiscretions of various units on the subject of intelligence and secrecy. The CO had carefully gone through his office copy noting in the margin against various items the action to be taken. The GOC suddenly waxed very wrath on reading this copy, and suddenly turning to the CO said 'What, Sir, do you mean by writing the word "Balls" against certain items in my instructions?'

'That, Sir, was written against those parts of the instructions which I wished my orderly room clerk to attend to – his name happens to be Balls,' replied the CO.

Chapter 11

Major General Douglas Wimberley

Details

This section is a chapter from General Wimberley's memoirs which are held at the Imperial War Museum. Wimberley's military career began in the Officer Training Corps at Wellington and Cambridge University. He completed his military education at Sandhurst from December 1914 to May 1915, and was commissioned into the 3rd (Militia) Battalion Cameron Highlanders at Invergordon. He was transferred to the 1st Battalion and saw action with them at the Battle of Loos, October 1915. He transferred again, this time to the newly formed Machine Gun Corps, and saw action at the Somme, 1916, with the 1st and 2nd Brigade Machine Gun Companies. He saw action at 3rd Ypres (July to September 1917), the Somme (October 1917), and at Cambrai (November 1917). During 1918, he commanded the 51st Battalion, Machine Gun Corps. In 1919, he saw service in Russia, with the 8th Battalion, Machine Gun Corps, after which he returned to the Cameron Highlanders. Wimberley served in Ireland in County Cork with the Camerons during the War of Independence, returning afterwards to Aldershot. He served with the British Army of the Rhine from 1923 to 1925, time which included a spell at Cambridge University. He attended Staff College from 1926 to 1927. From 1928 to 1933, he served in India, including service in the 1st Indian (Gurkha) Infantry Brigade. He was attached to the Adjutant General and the Military Training Directorates of the War Office from 1934 to 1937. From 1938 to 1939, he commanded the 1st Battalion Cameron Highlanders. In 1940, he was placed in command of a temporary brigade earmarked for the capture of Stavanger in 1940. He held the command of the 13th Brigade (5th Division), the 152nd Brigade (51st Highland Division), before assuming the command of the 46th Division in Britain from 1940 to 1941. He took command of the 51st Highland Division, which fought in North Africa, taking part in the Battles of El Alamein, Medenine, the Mareth and Akarit Lines, and the conquest of Sicily. He served as Commandant of the Staff College, Camberley, from September 1943 to September 1944. From December 1944 to September 1946, he served as Director of Infantry at the War Office.

Ireland – 'The Trouble' (1920-1921)
I NOW DECIDED that I must try and get back to the Camerons, though I knew this meant dropping my Major's crown, which I had now worn, and drawn army pay for, during almost two years.

I set off to Aldershot, to see the 2nd Camerons there, and find out if the Home Battalion had any room for me. It was quite an ordeal. I had not been with the regiment since early 1916, and three years, in war time, is a long time. However, they were all very nice to me, particularly Donald Cameron, who had known me in the MG Corps at Gratham, and was now their very efficient Adjutant.

So I left the Machine Gun Corps and returned home to my regiment and found myself as a mere spare Captain in 'B' Company commanded by J McK. Gordon, whom I had served under in the same company of the 1st Battalion in France for a few weeks in 1915.

He was a strict disciplinarian, and could be touchy and choleric, but a first rate regimental officer.

Later I was to discover I had made the right decision. In 1919 we seconded officers were being urged to transfer to the MG Corps, and told thereby we would get quicker promotion; yet in a year or so the whole MG Corps was disbanded, MG's were once more given to Infantry Battalions to man, and most of the regular officers in that Corps drifted into the Tank Corps, amongst them Nasmith and Freddie Garrett.

I now enjoyed my time at Aldershot very much, as a spare captain I had little work to do, and very little responsibility, and after five years of war, and war conditions, it was a very pleasant interlude.

The commanding officer was George Sorel-Cameron, who certainly looked the part. Very smart and well turned out, and with a good word of command, he was a fine horsemen. He was as straight as a dye, and was popular with all ranks. He had been a prisoner almost all the war, and being a slow thinker, he did not know much about what was then up to date soldiering.

The second-in-command was Aldecron, one of the very few Regular Army English officers we had in the Camerons. He, too, was a very popular if eccentric officer, with a gallant war record. He had been shot through the head in the Boer War, and we thought, rightly or wrongly, this was what accounted for his eccentricities.

The then Regimental Sergeant Major was a great character, 'Big Jimmie' Templeton, DCM, from Kinloch Rannoch. A fine figure of a six foot Highlander, and at one time a deer stalker, with a splendid war record. He was though, unfortunately, a hard drinker. He was a magnificent RSM of the old type, whereby all the soldiers felt to see that their Glengarry was cocked at the right regimental angle, and all their brass buttons were correctly done up, when he was seen a hundred yards away.

Our own Company Sergeant Major was Neil McCaskill, DCM,

a fine character, and a west coast gaelic speaking Highlander from the island of Bernera. He spoke his English in the Gaelic idiom usually beginning all sentences with the words, 'I wasss thinking ...'

I could not have had around me a nicer lot of officer contemporaries of my own age, most of whom were to be my great friends for life. Owing to the recent war, we were all substantive captains, so with our war medals and decorations, and the experience that went with them, there was bound to be a considerable gulf between us, and the few young subalterns in the Battalion who had seen little or no active service.

We called ourselves, in fun, the 'Captains' Union', and if Donald Cameron, the Adjutant, put us on duty in the afternoon, we used to protest vociferously; though I may say quite without avail.

There was Angus Collier, later to be best man at my wedding, as I was at his; some day to become a major general. There was Phil Christison, later to command a Corps in much Burma fighting, to be C-in-C Scotland and a Knight Cross of the British Empire. Colin Cameron, a fine all round athlete, who was later to do splendid work for the regiment as retired officer at our depot at Cameron Barracks, Inverness. Pringle-Pattison, or PP as he was universally known, my companion at the Stirling nursing home, son of a distinguished professor of philosophy at the University of Edinburgh; and Ian Maxwell, a Catholic, whose mother was a Lovat Fraser, a most pleasant companion, but to whom punctuality meant nothing, much to the worry of his faithful CSM.

When I first rejoined the regiment, also serving at Aldershot was Puggie Stewart of Kinlochmoidart, who had command of a Battalion with distinction in Salonika at a very early age, and Lawrence Sloane, DFC, our best athlete, who had also played rugby football for Scotland, but these two were shortly to retire still as regimental captains; I did not therefore get to know them as well as the others.

But if we had but little work to do at this period, this certainly did not apply to games and athletics. Except at weekends, almost every afternoon saw us playing strenuous rugby or hockey, and most of us were in strict training with the Jocks. About two days a week we were all herded into the gymnasium after the mess dinner where we were put through vigorous physical training by the RSM himself.

It was entirely due to the RSM Templeton that I achieved some prowess as a runner, a sport I had never cared for, and never attempted since my Sandhurst days. Every Saturday morning, the entire unit were ordered on a cross-country run, except those over the age of 30. We were gradually graded into packs according to our ability, and after a few weeks I found myself promoted to the fast pack, in which were the Battalion cross country runners. In a month or so, I found myself detailed for the Army and Command Cross Country races; gruelling affairs that afforded me no pleasure, and, in addition, picked too for the regiment in the half mile and mile.

In the rugby fifteen we played the maximum number of officers then allowed, which was eight, as except for our handful of Borderer Jocks from Hawick, Selkirk and the like towns, none of our men had ever played the rugby code. In the football team, on the other hand, no officer from the regiment was good enough to play in the first eleven, with the sole exception of David Macdonald, the charming son of a famous Cameron major and quartermaster, who had been at George Watson's school and played football there.

Thanks to the encouragement of the Adjutant, Donald Cameron, and the drive of the RSM, we, the Camerons, soon became very successful at all games and sports at Aldershot, winning many competitions, which at once did much to raise the morale of our Jocks, and make them proud of their regiment.

So, for me, some halcyon months passed by, only interrupted by a few small alarms. At one time we were under definite orders to go at short notice to Memel in East Prussia on the Baltic to supervise a plebiscite, and optimistic as the young always are, most of us at once laid in large stocks of shot gun cartridges for the geese, and wild fowling, which was reported to be very good in those parts. However, at the last minute, and after our advance party had already left, the move for some reason or other was cancelled.

It was really the first time, in all my six years spent in soldiering, that I had lived in a peace time Mess of the Regular Army, and this, too, I found very pleasant, after years of war and active service.

In those days the ante-room was closed to officers for half an hour before Mess dinner to let the waiters tidy up and open windows, etc., while we officers bathed and put on mess kit, and the tight strapped trews, this of course included stiff white shirts. When we gathered in the mess room, summoned by the Orderly piper, no smoking was allowed, and sherry and bitters was the normal ante-room drink.

We then walked in behind the senior officer dining, and sat down to a five course dinner. As soon as the port wine had circulated, officers were free to leave the table, but most nights of the week we sat on and talked for, maybe, another half hour. Mess dinner every night was, therefore, a leisurely affair, lasting in all anything up to a couple of hours.

To drink beer or stout at mess was unheard of, though one could of course drink water, as was smoking a pipe, even in the ante-room. I think most of us drank whiskey and soda, and a few brandy and soda. In those days this was not expensive. Spirits were always served to each officer, already mixed with soda, in a small glass mug, which was allowed on the table. No wine bottle, however, was ever allowed to rest on the table, and was put on the floor at the person's foot.

Needless to say, no ladies' name was ever mentioned in mess or ante-room, and military 'shop', though allowed in the ante-room, was not encouraged at the mess table. I am, now, sometimes asked by young officers, what we talked about night after night in Mess. It is difficult to remember, but my recollection is that we covered a wide field. I suppose, in those days, a third of us were university men, and certainly we, of the self called 'Captain's Union', who often sat together, had a wide range of interests.

Phil Christison was something of a naturalist, and was later to write a book on Indian birds. Angus Collier had always a hankering for ancient history.

Family history was already becoming a leisure hobby of mine. Again, thanks to the war, we had all travelled widely, and between us had covered the Western Front, Gallipoli, Salonika, East Africa and the Arctic. Again, most of us had common interests, as regards what 'Punch' used to term as 'huntin', shootin', and fishin''.

But, of course, the real bond linking us all was that we were intensely proud of our regiment, and its great record, and almost equally proud of the whole Highland Brigade.

To encourage the standard of piping in the regiment, we usually had the day's Orderly piper playing round the Mess table every night, except, of course, Sundays, when these was no Mess dinner, and a cold supper was served. Once a young Hebridean piper was playing in the Mess for the first time. When the time came for him to stand and play his strathspay and reel, he walked to the nearest corner of the room, firmly turned his back on us all at table, and played his tunes facing the wall. On being asked afterwards why he had done this, he replied: 'I was chust that nervous, I couldn't face all the chentlemen.'

In the late spring HM King George V, our Colonel in Chief of the Camerons, visited Aldershot, and stayed in the Royal Pavilion, Aldershot then being a military station where no less than two Divisions had their Headquarters and the bulk of their 24 Infantry Battalions were actually stationed. He held a Review on Laffans

Plain, and I had the honour of marching past my company, as the massed pipes played the *Pibroch O'Dhomnuill Dubh*.

In May 1920, we received sudden orders to move to County Cork in Southern Ireland; then the storm centre of what was known in Ireland as 'the troubles'. We travelled by sea from Southampton in the HMT *Czaritea*, the same ship that had taken me a year before to Archangel, and the stewards in the saloon assured me we ate exactly the same menus as in 1919. At that time, soon after the Great War and with some rationing still in force, the food seemed to us, of the 8th MG Battalion, as excellent; now, a year later and used to an excellent peacetime officer's mess in Aldershot, we rated the menus as rather indifferent. Life is always so much a mere matter of comparisons.

On arrival in Ireland our Battalion headquarters moved into a camp called Belmont Hutments, at Queenstown, now called Cobh, and we found outlying detachments in such places as Ballincollig, Middleton, Killeagh and Youghal. All around us those who were now called our enemies, the Sinn Féiners, all wore plain clothes, had their arms hidden, and spoke good English.

It was very difficult for some weeks to teach the Jocks that we were now in what was largely a hostile country, and that maybe 75 per cent of all local inhabitants, both men and women, viewed us with enmity, active or passive; though these sentiments were largely hidden.

We had to learn our job the hard way. Very soon after our arrival an unsuspecting road patrol, with their rifles stupidly clipped on to the side of their bicycles, were surrounded in a village street by a number of young men supposedly playing a game of hurley on the village green, a game akin to our own Highland Shinty. They apparently made friendly remarks and gestures, and gradually closed in on the cyclists. A few seconds later they had knocked the Jocks off their bicycles with their hurley sticks, and held up the men with revolvers. They removed the rifles' ammunition and bicycles of the soldiers, and they released them to return, under the NCO in charge, to our camp, very ashamed.

During the next few weeks, while moving about the Irish roads between our various detachments, small parties of our Battalion were ambushed and some men were killed and wounded, and one officer, a young subaltern, Ian Begg, by seizing the wheel from a wounded driver beside him, and though badly wounded himself, managed to drive his vehicle right through an ambush at high speed, for this he was later given an MBE.

Then occurred an even worse rebuff to our pride. Another young officer, with a small working party, was ordered to demolish an army hut in Queenstown. He very unwisely ordered his men to pile their arms, and then put them to work with picks and shovels some 30 yards or so away from their firearms. The job took him several days and, worst of all, he followed exactly the same practise each day.

On the third or fourth day, while the party were at their work, a volley of shots suddenly rang out. The sentry over the arms fell a casualty, several Sinn Féiners then jumped out of the windows of the ground floor of some houses close by, and covered the surprised workers with rifles, shot guns and revolvers, and meanwhile a motor van drove up close to the piked arms, and a Sinn Féiner or two bundled them up into the motor and drove off.

The whole Battalion felt very angry and ashamed that day. We, a famous regiment, had lost ten or twelve rifles to the rebels with but one casualty, the sentry; and without our having fired a shot. However, we were now learning our lesson, that we must be ever vigilant of all local Irish, and all were our enemy unless we knew them to be otherwise.

Thereafter we lost no more arms, and soon we began in our turn to capture hidden arms and to inflict casualties on our hidden plain clothes enemy. It was, however, most frustrating and unpleasant work for us all, and certainly we soldiers felt that we were not being given a free enough hand by Parliament to deal with the situation with which we were faced.

Soon after the fiasco in Queenstown when our working party lost all their rifles, the soldiers discovered that two girls, daughters of a loyalist, who had attended a troop's dance had had all their hair shaved off by local Sinn Féiners for so doing, as a reprisal for their behaviour. This was reported to the civil authorities, but no action was taken, and indeed practically the whole civil and police authority had already broken down.

In Youghal, a middle-aged married policeman of the Royal Irish Constabulary was shot in the back as he came out of Catholic Mass in the town. I happened to be near at the time, and though as the shot rang out the streets were full of people, they all hurriedly left. The man was just left to die on the street. I and one or two with me were left to carry him, a dying man, into a local chemist's shop.

Our NCOs and men, and indeed some of our young officers, felt that we should be allowed to take much sterner action with the rebels. Many cases had arisen of obvious Sinn Féiners having been arrested and tried, but if they had managed to hide or dispose of their arms and automatics, they were as often as not acquitted and released. On the other hand if the troops fired on and wounded a civilian, or killed him, whatever were the circumstances, a dozen civilian witnesses were always ready to come forward and state that the man concerned was invariably one of the most loyal inhabitants in all County Cork, and as often as not the unfortunate officer or NCO in charge of the army party concerned would then receive an official reprimand, while the local Irish press fulminated over the action of the brutal and licentious Cameron Highlanders.

Matters came more and more to a head, and the troops became more and more restive, and chafed at the restraints they were invariably subjected to. Finally, one night, a report came to the CO, while we officers were all dining in Mess, that the Camerons were loose in the town of Queenstown breaking the windows of all the shops. By this time I was Assistant Adjutant and, as such, I was sent out in a great hurry to investigate.

It was true enough, I soon ran into a party of some 50 NCOs and men, under the RSM himself. They were armed only with tools' wooden handles, and they were systematically and deliberately breaking every shop window as they passed by. They were all quite sober, but the Jocks had felt that they were not being allowed to deal properly with their enemies, and they sensed, and rightly, that many of the inhabitants of Queenstown were reporting their every movement to the local Sinn Féin bands, and they had therefore decided they would retaliate. I sternly ordered them to return to camp at once, and back they came with me now at their head, but still, I fear, rather pleased with themselves and they rather reminded me of a pack of naughty dogs caught out in forbidden rabbit hunting.

Well, there was, of course, the 'father and mother' of a row over the incident. The Divisional General, Sir Peter Strickland, 'Old Hungry Face' as the soldiers called him, I believe, had the whole Battalion paraded, and what the Army calls 'told us off to no uncertain tune'. In his eyes we were indisciplined and insubordinate, and I believe our CO, Sorel Cameron, was nearly removed from commanding us.

However, the Jocks had let off steam, and in point of fact their indisciplined action really did a lot of good, for the military authorities were forced to realise that the troops were not prepared to stand, any more, a policy of never being supported, whatever politicians in London might be advocating.

After that unfortunate incident we officers took care whenever what was called an 'Incident', as skirmishes were then called, or when policemen were murdered, which involved Cameron Highlanders, we at once worked the troops off their legs for the next 48 hours, searching and patrolling for the culprits for miles into the countryside, until all our soldiers wanted to do was a chance to sleep; and by this time tempers had cooled.

Of all duties we were called upon to do, I think, the searching of houses was the most distasteful and unpleasant. To start with most of them were literally swarming with fleas, which we then invariably picked up, and as soon as I got back to camp I used to bathe and change my clothes. In one house, which I was searching I myself found in the floor, under a loose floor board, a cavity in which a revolver was probably hidden. The rebel and his pistol was not at home, but in the hiding place was a real hymn of hate poem. I have still a copy of it and it ran for many verses. The first verse began:

God curse the British Empire.
May he wither the flag that flies
May he shatter the strength that still remains
Of that father of sin and lies
May he strengthen the hands of its enemies
May he hasten its dying gasp
May Satan rise from the depths of Hell
That ulcer of earth to grasp.

And so on in the same strain for six more verses.

About this time, we, as a Battalion, started in Queenstown an unjust collective measure, which from our point of view, however, soon bore good results. One day, without any warning, we rounding up and brought compulsorily into Camp at Belmont, which was surrounded with barbed wire, all the males whom we found anywhere in the streets of the town. They amounted to several hundred men. We made no exceptions whatever, and so those collected, much to their fury, were well known loyalists as well as suspected Sinn Féiners and included several retired officers of the British Army.

Once safely shepherded inside our camp and our sentries, we paraded them all together, and took the names and addresses of every man, using local Royal Irish Constabulary policemen, as necessary, to help identification when we thought any individual might be giving a false name. We then and there detailed them haphazardly, in small groups of five and six, as being 'on duty' for every night of the next month or two.

We explained to them through a megaphone, as the present loudspeakers had not been invented then or at any rate were not yet in use, as to what being on duty entailed. It meant, we explained, that if a hostile incident occurred within the town boundaries of Queenstown, whereby any member of the Camerons, or the police, were killed or wounded, we would at once arrest and hold and incarcerate in a cage of wire in our camp, all those half dozen civilians that we had detailed for duty for that 24 hours.

Now this meant that those concerned had either to leave their homes and 'go on the run', as it was then called, in a hurry, or else wait in their homes till we collected them and then incarcerated them. By this arrangement, we calculated, that it was now probable that in the five or six men concerned, in any 24 hours, at least one of them would probably have some influence with the local town Sinn Féin leaders, and he would do his best to dissuade his friends from carrying out an incident against us during the period we had arbitrarily detailed his for duty and possible arrest. I may say this plan worked, so far as the town of Queenstown was concerned, surprisingly well.

Nevertheless, as the months passed by, more and more of the unfortunate policemen of the Royal Irish Constabulary were killed in action, or more often shot down and murdered. The survivors naturally became very nervous, and the morale of the force quite disappeared. Soon they would no longer identify suspicious rebels we produced before them, as they knew that to do so meant revenge, and generally death later for them, as, living as they were in little isolated police stations in the various towns and villages, there was no way in which we could arrange to protect them adequately.

We therefore used to arrange to parade our prisoners in the courtyard of our guard room, and we secreted a local RIC constable where he could see the prisoners through a small peep hole, but the prisoners did not know they were being so watched.

It was by this method that we were able to get identified the local 'Robin Hood', a man named Henry O'Mahony who had, on capture, given us a false name. He was a colourful character, and the local Sinn Féin leader in our area. We had him imprisoned in a fort on Spike Island, a small island in the Cork Harbour, but he soon escaped by means of a disused passage into the fort's moat. I think we had a sneaking admiration for him, for though very ruthless, there rebels were certainly brave, and, according to their beliefs, patriotic men.

One way in which we tried to obtain information of rebel activities was by using our Gaelic speakers. Some of the rebels knew Irish Gaelic, and those that did used it for reasons of secrecy. We accordingly sent our west coast Highlanders into public houses to listen, but the Irish Gaelic was so different to the Highland Gaelic that I do not think anything was achieved.

We knew that every telephone conversation was invariably tapped, as most of the post office workers were Sinn Féin sympathisers, but over this we were sometimes able to turn the situation to our advantage, as we deliberately reported in conversations by telephone, small troop movements well in advance, which we hoped thereby would be ambushed on route, and we, in our turn laid ambushed for the expected ambushers.

As the months went by matters seemed to get worse and worse in Ireland, and there was little relaxation for either officers or men. We officers were able to play golf on the local links, but it was an order that we had to play in two foursomes one behind the other, and all eight of us armed with revolvers in our pockets. At first some officers used to go out hunting with the local foxhounds, but soon this was at an end.

During the Troubles lost ammunition usually meant ammunition stolen by the rebels, and accordingly to lose ammunition was a serious offence. Before I went into the orderly room, one of the Jocks in my company lost five rounds of rifle ammunition, and in consequence our Brigadier, Higginson, not only had him punished, but also ordered my leave, as the OC Company, to be stopped! Later all leave for officers, was stopped for a time; I think it was after a lot of officers had been murdered one night in Dublin. This hit me hard as my father arranged to go with me to Shetland to fish, and fishing and accommodation was all booked.

As Assistant Adjutant, one of my duties was to help the Adjutant, Donald Cameron, to keep the Secret Files and documents. One of these files was called 'Prominent Sinn Féiners', and in it were photos and dossiers and descriptions of such men as de Valera, Michael Collins and the like; men whom at the time we were trying to capture. This was regarded as a very secret file, and, as such, when not in use had to be kept in the orderly room safe.

One day in September 1920, Donald went off to the mess for luncheon before me, and took with him the safe key, the file was not locked up, as I had been studying it, and as I did not like to leave it in the orderly room untended I decided to take it with me to the mess.

In the middle of lunch, a signal message was suddenly delivered to the CO, or more likely the Adjutant on his behalf, with the welcome news that leave had been reopened. I had already lost several days of my fishing, and I did not waste time. I changed into plain clothes and caught the night train to Dublin that afternoon.

I frankly found it a frightening journey. I travelled with my .45

Brigadier Higginson, the Commander of the 17th Infantry Brigade, inspecting Ballinhassig RIC Barracks, County Cork.

Colt automatic in one pocket, and another .32 automatic in the other. Not long before some British officers had been pulled out of a train, in cold blood and shot. Every time the train stopped I felt nervous and alone. Every time a ticket collector came to the compartment, while I showed him my ticket with one hand, I kept the other in my pocket on the butt of one or other pistol. Nothing happened at all, and soon I was safely on the boat travelling from Dublin to Holyhead, but I decided I was not cut out for lone intelligence work, I was too frightened.

From Holyhead, I travelled by train north to Perth and then to Aberdeen. Here I caught the Lerwick steamer, and there I changed into a very small steamer called the *Earl of Zetland* which went to the Northern Isles. It deposited me at Balta Sound on the Isle of Unst, the most northerly island of all, in the early hours of one morning. I had been travelling for about three days and nights.

My father met me, and in his hand was a telegram already waiting for me. It was short and to the point: 'Report whereabouts of File SX 40 or return forthwith'. I knew the file of course, but for some minutes I could not, for the life of me, remember what I had done with it. Then it all came back to me, and I wired back: 'Quartermaster's Stores, search fleabag'. I had pushed the secret file down to the bottom of my bedding role to hide it, in the mess, while I lunched, as I slept in the small mess building. Then, in my excitement at getting way on leave, I had forgotten all about it and told my soldier servant to roll up my bedding and to put it in the Stores.

I had a splendid fishing holiday, mainly in Loch Cliff, for sea trout, fishing almost under the shadow of the Muckle Flugga Lighthouse, the most northerly building in Great Britain. When not fishing we picniced with Mother, and spent hours watching all the sea birds, and in particular the Great Skuas, the boldest birds in Britain, so far as man is concerned. From Unst we moved to Bridge of Walls on the main island, here the actual sea trout fishing was better than further north, so we went back there in September 1922, and as my fishing skill improved, I got several fine sea trout of three or so pounds.

Soon after I got back from my leave, Donald Cameron left us for six months leave to his home at Forden in Tasmania, and so I became acting Adjutant. I think, as it was, our Brigadier, Higginson, knew his job well enough, but he was certainly well served, for his Brigade Major was Brevet Lieutenant Colonel Montgomery, 'Monty' now to all Britain, and his Staff Captain was the brother of 'Bimbo' Dempsey later to command the whole British Army in Normandy and Germany in the Second World War.

In September, 1921 they decided to hold a Brigade Sports meeting in Cork, and at that time there were about eight infantry regiments in the 17th Cork Brigade. Travelling to and from sports meetings and inter-unit games at that period was an unusual affair. We conveyed to and from in old fashioned motor vehicles, covered with rabbit netting to keep out any Sinn Féin grenades thrown at us, and all armed, to the teeth, with Lewis guns, rifles and grenades.

From the regiment's point of view this athletic meeting was a great success, as we won the championship cup given, and it was also satisfactory that, out of all the regiments competing, the only other Scots regiment, our friends of the KOSB, were the runners up.

I acted as captain of our team, and won one or two races myself, for which I got the silver cigarette box I still have. I don't think, though, I can have been a very good captain in some ways, because it seems I appointed myself to tell our best long distance runner, one Sergeant Herniman, the number of each lap he was running, as he passed me in a three mile track race. I used stones in my pocket to register the laps, but he has more than once reminded me, in recent years, that I managed to mix up my stones, and he kept his final sprint for a lap, after the winning post was reached, and thereby lost the race.

The great bulk of our Battalion went to Cork for this meeting and after we had won we marched through the streets of Cork playing the pipe tune 'The Black Bear' traditionally reserved for occasions like this, with all the Jocks 'hooching' away hard when the drums beat by themselves and the pipers stop for a few notes at regular intervals.

Soon after this meeting in, I think, October 1921, Donald Cameron, now back from Australia, was taken away from us to be a Brigade Major at Aldershot, and I succeeded him as the proper gazetted Adjutant. I was very pleased at this, as Adjutant was by far the best job any junior officer could hold, and my own grandfather had been Adjutant of the 79th Cameron Highlanders some 60 odd years before me. Donald was eight years older than I was, he was already a Brevet Major, who had passed through the Staff College. He was one of the few serving officers who had joined before 1914 as a regular, and was a man we all liked and respected, and some I knew feared, and not without just cause.

I was to be the Adjutant for over three and half years, all told, and I much enjoyed my time in this appointment. There is no doubt that, in my day, he cut a far more important figure in an Infantry Battalion than is the case today. There was apparently far less office work than nowadays, and in any case I nearly always contrived to have an unofficial Assistant Adjutant, in the office, who took most of the dull routine work off my shoulders.

I thus had the time, and accepted the opportunity now allowed me, to interest myself and meddle in any side of the Battalion's activities that I cared to. One of my main interests was regimental history, and I took all the piper, drummer, tradesmen and band boys in this subject, myself, every week, as well as lecturing all the NCOs. We had, in those days, between twenty and 30 boys in the unit. They had all enlisted for long service and most of them eventually did their 21 years in the Army, ending often as our Warrant Officers.

I must admit my teaching of Army history was biased in the extreme, always extolling the Highland Brigade in general, and the Camerons in particular! The object of course was to arouse still further the intense regimental esprit of these lads.

The type of question given them was therefore generally as follows: 'What do you know about the assault on Burgos in 1812?' Answer expected: ... 'The first man to enter the hornwork of the fortress was Sergeant John Mackenzie of the 79th' ... Question: 'Which Division after Waterloo, did Wellington particularly commend in his despatch?' Answer expected: ... 'The 5th Division in which were serving all the Highland regiments' ... and so on. I also took care, on every battle anniversary in which the regiment had distinguished itself, to insert in the day's orders a short account of the part we played.

Another particular interest of mine were the young NCOs. It so happened that, during much of my tenure, several of the Company Commanders were Brevet Lieutenant Colonels, who had even commanded Battalions in the Great War. As a result, they found it difficult to enthuse over the training and administration of a weak infantry company in barracks at Aldershot. Provided, therefore, they were outwardly deferred to, and consulted, they were prepared to leave the Adjutant with a very free hand. It is no exaggeration to say that few if any private soldiers ever asked for promotion to Lance Corporal, without first being picked out and then told to apply by the Adjutant.

Again every NCO going temporarily away, say on a course of instruction, was seen alone by the Adjutant and exhorted, when away from us, to be a good Cameron, and thus a pattern of smartness and efficiency. Every NCO going on leave was again interviewed by me and instructed exactly how to set about enlisting more Camerons while at home, and thus claim and get the extra leave and regimental reward of money he earned thereby. After every Battalion drill parade, the RSM brought up directly in front of me, as Adjutant, any soldiers who had been deemed as idle on parade. I, there and then, awarded them, I may say quite illegally, extra drill parades, and did this without any reference to their company commanders.

Similarly all minor punishments of subaltern officers lay in the Adjutant's hands. Each offender was always asked ... 'Will you take the punishment awarded ... (which usually entailed extra spells of doing orderly officer or stoppage of leave) ... or do you want to be reported to the Commanding Officer?' In practise the last procedure was seldom necessary. If the wise CO ever noticed that Lieutenant 'X' seemed to remain a lot in barracks, and was more often than others on some regimental duty, he just held his peace.

In addition, I found being Adjutant in Southern Ireland was an unusual appointment for a soldier, and often very hard work. As the whole civil administration of the country had broken down and ceased to work, a sort of martial law was in force. As a result we in the orderly room, for instance, had to take on the local registration of births, deaths and marriages, and even hold all the inquests, of which, at such a time, there were certainly plenty.

I well remember one occasion when I, and my Assistant Adjutant, Alasdair Macgillivray, later on retirement to become a well known Baillie of Inverness, held an inquest in the orderly room, on the body of a new born infant, who had been found suffocated with a rag in its throat, close to our camp. He and I held many other rather macabre inquests as well as this one, when we had the poor baby's body on the orderly room table.

Another inquest I held was in a village nearby called Carrigtwowell, on the corpse of a man, who was laid out in a cottage surrounded by lighted candles, while a lot of Irish women were holding a wake, and wailing around the body. I came to the conclusion that the man had been murdered by some opposing Irish faction and I returned a verdict of death by unknown hand. Many years later it was revealed to me that the man had in fact been shot, or even murdered, by a certain Cameron, who had been out on his own secretly at night. I think the madman concerned was the same individual who was soon after removed from the regiment and the Army.

This sort of thing was the seamy side of Ireland as far as the British were concerned. I am sure it happened because the British Government would not, or dare not, properly support the Army in the impossible task they had given it to do, tied as we were always by restrictions on our legal actions.

Finally, as matters became really bad, the Government brought into Southern Ireland irregular volunteer forces of semi-soldiers and semi-police called 'Black and Tans', who were largely recruited all over Britain from ex-temporary officers and men who had served in the Great War, of a type who would not, or could not, settle down in civil life, and some of whom were undoubtedly no more or less than real 'thugs'. They were totally undisciplined, by our regimental standards, and members of this curious force undoubtedly committed many atrocities, and, in retaliation, dreadful atrocities were, in turn, committed on them by the Sinn Féin bands roaming the countryside.

They seemed to make a habit of breaking out of their barracks at night, illicitly, and killing men they thought were suspect rebels, and in this way the habit spread surreptitiously even to a few Army officers and men. So indisciplined were some of these auxiliary policemen, who had been recruited to reinforce the remnants of the Royal Irish Constabulary, most of whom had by this time been killed, that whenever some of them accompanied me, on any search, patrol or foray, in which I was in command, my first action was always to detail two or three of my Jocks simply to watch over them, and see that they did not commit any atrocities such as unlawfully looting or burning houses, when they were acting under my command, or even shooting prisoners, on the grounds that they were attempting to escape.

Nevertheless, despite all that I have recounted, we, young officers, managed to have quite a lot of fun in Ireland. We had, for instance, a number of jolly guest nights; with very few exceptions we were never the least drunk, but we were full of fun, and enjoyed after dinner wild Reel dancing and riotous games.

At one dinner we had as chief guest, Admiral Sir Reginald Tupper, then Naval C in C at Queenstown, of what was then called the Western Approaches. He was a splendid old sportsman, and seemed to thoroughly enjoy his time with us. After dinner we got him into the middle of a rather wild eightsome reel, and once in the centre we never let him out; each one of us in turn 'hooched' the old chap, and did our reel steps to him, which he nobly tried to follow. At the end, he was naturally very exhausted, and some of us felt rather penitent, as he was really too old for such wild ploys. Rumour had it when he got back to Admiralty House he was put to bed for a day or two by Lady Tupper to recuperate!

Again, at that period, we had various small detachments in the various forts in Cork Harbour, such as Fort Carlisle and Campden. Visiting them gave us opportunities for good mackerel fishing. At Youghal the sea fishing seemed to be very good, and once when stationed there, we went out fishing with the local doctor, and anchored to fish. I was very sick indeed in the Atlantic swell and did not at all enjoy it.

After some months Admiral Tupper left and was succeeded by Admiral Sir Ernest Gaunt; with Admiral Tupper went his daughter, a most popular young lady with the youngsters of both services. Admiral Gaunt arranged a big fancy dress at Admiralty House to which all Camerons were invited. Here all could dance in safety, as the naval residence was surrounded by armed marine sentries, and a Marine band played.

Now we soldiers were, of course, on semi-active service, and had little kit with us. After dining in the Mess one night, therefore, we all dressed ourselves up as best we could, using sporran tassels as imitation beards, and putting on collars back to front to represent clerical dress, etc. We then set off to Admiralty House in good spirits, well pleased with our efforts. This attitude did not last long. We were received by the Admiral and his lady, both of whom were in resplendent professional costumes; the Admiral togged up as King Henry VIII or some such costume. Then, we found all around us Naval officers who had taken the fancy dress ball very seriously, and moving about as they did, in their ships, were all dressed in real fancy dresses hired in London, from places like Clarksons. We had made a very poor showing and felt, now, rather embarrassed.

That night, the Battalion orderly officer was a Second Lieutenant Alasdair Maclean of Pennycross in Mull. Shortly before I left for the ball, he knocked on my door, already dressed up in some weird fancy dress, and asked for my permission, as Adjutant, to get a non-dancing officer to answer for him in barracks. I, naturally, as Adjutant ordered him straight back to duty, and told him to report to me again in five minutes properly dressed in uniform. The next day I said to him, 'Alasdair, why on earth did you not come to me and ask for leave to exchange duty properly dressed in uniform; if you had I would certainly have let you exchange, but coming, as you did, was just too much for any self-respecting Adjutant'. His answer was, 'I just thought you would not have the heart to stop me, when you saw me all beautifully dressed up'. Perhaps with that rather unusual outlook for a soldier, it is not surprising that my friend Alasdair has ended up as a wonderful producer of Army Tattoos, for which work all Scotland knows about him.

At one time in Ireland I was living in a partitioned hut, divided by match-boarding into a number of small sleeping rooms. Mine happened to be at the end next to where several of the officers' batmen were wont to collect when cleaning our uniforms. One evening I lay on my bed, and heard several of the Jocks talking away, and with the thin partitioning, short of blocking my ears, I could hear every word said. They had got hold of an old Army List which they were thumbing through at our regimental page. As each name was read out, some Jock or other would remark ... 'Och, I know yon man' and then proceed to make a short pithy remark on the officer in question.

Generally, in their remarks it seemed to me, while kindly disposed to our foibles, they were very much 'on target', and I thought how little the soldiers missed regarding the strengths and weaknesses of their officer's characters. Finally they got to one of my brother officer's names, a nice man, but certainly ineffectual. The reader of his name dismissed him with but one short contemptuous remark ... 'Ach, Haskett, he's no an officer at all, at all, the poor mannie, chust a choke'.

As was natural, as the Sinn Féin movement gradually gathered strength, fewer and fewer of the local Irish families attempted to entertain Army officers from a very natural fear of reprisals; but a definite local exception was the family of the well known local bank manager, belonging to an old Irish Roman Catholic family. He had several daughters, and very good looking and charming girls they were, and so partly due to his courageous attitude, at one period three of his daughters became engaged to no less than three of our Protestant Cameron officers. Later two of these engagements ended in marriage, to my great friend Colin Cameron, and to Charlie Macleod (Dalvey), son of the old Dalvey, who commanded a company in the 3rd Battalion when I joined at Invergorden, some seven years earlier.

As regards the soldiers, there is no doubt but at this time, a good deal of hard drinking went on, especially in the Sergeants' Mess, and it was no wonder, for when off duty there was so little for them to do, cooped up as we were in a small camp surrounded by sentries and barbed wire. We did our best with games in camp and whist drives and the like, but we were allowed no wives or families there, and few of the local Irish girls dared to be seen with a British soldier.

I had an old orderly room clerk sergeant whom I knew very well was a hard drinker, though one never saw him drunk. Suddenly the poor man went sick, and it was finally diagnosed as lead poisoning. The cause was that in the Sergeants' Mess there was a lead pipe from the beer barrel, in which the first pint drawn off, spent the night. He was invariably the first man to drink a pint in the morning, hence his illness.

When New Year's Day came, I, as Adjutant, ordered double guards and sentries all round our perimeter wire, as knowing what would happen inside camp it seemed an obvious precaution. All the various companies had the usual tremendous New Years' dinners, and as Adjutant I had to go round with the Commanding Officer and drink a toast of neat whisky, to the officers and men of each company.

As a result of this, and a heavy midday meal, I was just settling down to a New Year's afternoon nap, when the Brigade Headquarters phoned me up, (it was probably Monty), as Brigade Major, himself) and gave orders that a large party was to be sent out at once in our lorries, to hunt for a suspected ambush, or some such ploy, ten or twenty miles away.

Now normally we always had a platoon on duty for an instant job like this, and all one did was to order the Guard Bugler to sound three 'G's' on his bugle and the duty party turned out at the double, while the duty lorries warmed their engines. Now the RSM and I had already picked some 50 well known teetotallers that day as all the camp guards, and I felt that to order out the standby duty troops at 3pm on New Year's day might be tricky for the officers concerned. I decided, therefore, to sound the camp fire alarm, whereby every single officer and man in camp had to fall in at the double on parade. Several hundred men turned out, a good few in no shape for any lorried patrol, and I selected a composite force there and then from all the remaining teetotallers.

At last the British Government in July 1921 decided to treat and compromise with the rebel leaders. To my mind this was the only sensible course left open to them, for though no doubt we, in the Army, given the powers of life and death, and official policy of ruthlessness, could easily have quelled the actual active Sinn Féin revolt, by means of really stern measures backed by the British Government, I feel certain the discontent would have merely smouldered underground. It would have burst into flames as soon as we withdrew. The really brutal measures which Cumberland and his Army took in Scotland in 1745, finally to crush the rising there, would never have been tolerated by public opinion in Britain in 1921!

Soon after the Armistice, or truce, in Ireland, we, of the Camerons, were ordered back to Aldershot, and I do not think a single officer or man was sorry to leave the, so called, Emerald Isle behind us. Before we left Ireland, we were once more paraded by General Strickland in Belmont Hutments, and this time he was most complimentary in his remarks, on the part of we had played, and our spirit and morale. A few days later we embarked on a troop-ship in Cork Harbour on one of the most stormy nights of the whole year.

Once more we were back at peacetime soldiering, but after the Great War, North Russia, and then Southern Ireland, I had got so used to sleeping with a loaded pistol under my pillow, I found it quite difficult to drop the habit for many a month to come.

CHAPTER 12

Lieutenant Colonel Hughes-Hallett

Detail

This account is taken from the personal papers of the Lt Colonel Hughes-Hallett, and concerns his service with the King's Shropshire Light Infantry in Ireland from 1919 to 1922. He joined the British Army in September 1914, enlisting in the 9th Battalion Worcestershire Regiment at Tidworth, Wiltshire. His training as a junior officer began in October 1914, when he joined the 7th Battalion King's Shropshire Light Infantry. He served in France and Belgium during the First World War, and as a company commander at the Ypres salient from 1915 to 1916. He was seriously wounded in the Battle of Bazentin Ridge in 1916. After his service in Ireland, he was a company commander with the 1st Battalion KSLI in India from March 1925 to February 1934, serving at Poona, Dinapore, Muzaffapore, Razmak, Rawalpindi and Kuldana. During the Second World War, he was on garrison duty in Bermuda and in the Netherlands West Indies.

With 2/KSLI in Ireland 1919 to 1922

I JOINED THE 2nd Battalion at Fermoy, County Cork, in August 1919, from half-pay, and served with them in various stations until early 1922. Fermoy had been a pre-war station for the regiment and a number of regimental wives came from there. It had, I gathered, always been a happy station. One of my uncles had commanded his regiment there and my sisters had much enjoyed visiting their aunt and family there. When I first arrived, all seemed to be at peace – tennis parties and so forth in the surrounded country. Then – one Sunday – while the main body of the Battalion was falling-in in front of the Church, after Church parade, a hatless soldier rushed up calling out that he had a message for the CO. After being jumped on(!) by the RSM, he was fortunately seen by the CO, who called him up. His story was that he was one of the Wesleyan Party, going to their chapel in Patrick Street, some 'baker's dozen' strong. As they filed into the chapel doorway (he was the last man in the file and a cross-country runner) a gang of locals, sitting lounging around – in ambush – on various walls, suddenly produced revolvers and 'loaded' staves from their sleeves, and opened up on the backs of the troops at point blank range. The troops were carrying their rifles (for safety, just as was the custom in India), but no ammunition. One soldier (Private Lloyd) was killed on the spot and the rest knocked down. Their assailants seized their rifles (thirteen, I think) and drove off towards Cork (where they had come from). Trees, which had been sawn were pulled down to block the road from pursuit. All the houses round at once barricaded themselves in, and – except for the Wesleyan Minister and his wife – who did everything they could to help – not one soul was prepared to assist the injured men, even with a glass of water, although many of them must have known what was 'in the off'. The last soldier in the queue, who saw what was about to happen, knocked down several men and leapt the wall across the road, into the cattle market and ran to where he knew the battalion would be parading. As he ran through the built-up area he threw his rifle to an old woman ordering her to hide it. Hatless, he raced towards the Colonel. Lieutenant Norton was ordered to rush his platoon down into the town and round to the scene of the outrage; but it was too late. The murdering thugs had bolted. A coroner's inquest was ordered, and, owing to the machinations of a priest, it brought in a verdict of 'Accidental death, unpremeditated'. That was too much for the troops, many of whom were 'War' soldiers awaiting demobilisation. That evening we were at dinner in Mess, when the Mess Sergeant rushed in to say that 'The troops were in the town'.

The sound of breaking glass was heard, from the town, a few hundred yards away across the river (there was only the one bridge giving access). Everybody hurried to exchange mess-jacket for tweed coat and cap and hastened into the town. The Sergeant's Mess had been equally surprised and knew nothing of what was to occur. The troops had worked out a splendid plan. First they sent a screen ahead of the main body to clear the streets – ordering everybody, who was on foot, into their houses and to stay there. Then the demolition party proceeded to every shop or place of business of the coroner and the members of the jury, who had brought in their infamous verdict. I can't recall all the details, but the Jeweller (Barker?), the Boot Shop (Tyler), and the Wine Shop and particularly the foreman of the Jury, etc., were all faithfully dealt with. Trays of rings and watches were soon being flung into the river. A chain of men supervised by a captain, who was later to become Chief Constable of Devon, smashed bottles on the pavement, and drink flowed in a stream down the gutter. The Boot Shop produced one incident that could only be Irish. An old woman – looter – like jackals they had soon got wind of matters – had filled a sack with boots and shoes, but when she had reached the exit-door she realised she had no laces. She hurried back to collect some, only for another looter

A sergeant and private act as sentries in the signal box at Fermoy train station, County Cork, during the search of a train in February 1921.

to make-off with the sack. There she stood shouting for the police, as somebody was 'after stealing her boots'!! The fall-in was sounded at 10pm. Not a man was absent; and nobody was drunk. Next morning the Divisional Commander (Strickland) from Cork addressed the Battalion. He said we had had a damned dirty trick played on us and had had an adequate revenge. But enough was enough. It was his job to see that discipline was observed and that there would be no more. In the meanwhile the Battalion would be confined to Barracks. That was observed by all in the Regiment. However, that evening a large party of Gunners, who had not been privy to the first revenge, had spent the day making petrol torches etc., as they intended to burn down the Church of the offending priest. They assembled outside our barracks, while our men just sat on the wall. The Gunners kept calling 'What's the matter with the Shropshires? Aren't you coming with us?' But our people said 'No – they had done their bit'. Meanwhile I and Lieutenant Norton were sent on the double down to the town (leaving the barracks by a side exit; so the assembled Gunners would not see us go). Norton had to man the bridge over the river with fixed bayonets, I had to go into the town – clear St Patrick Street from end to end and keep it clear with my platoon in an open order of 4's (fixed bayonets) covering the road from pavement to pavement, and slowly sweep it clear, and keep it so. How long this lasted I can't recall, but at one time a senior RIC officer said to me that he hoped that the troops wouldn't get across the Bridge as at least 500 armed men had moved into the town during the day and were in every house round us and round the threatened Church!! I'm glad to say that they did not get across the Bridge!! The next move was that the Battalion, with Band and Colours, made a demonstration march thro' the town, it had been made very clear to the authorities that they had never yet apologised for the outrage and had not expressed one word of sorrow for the death of the soldier being killed in his

St Patrick's Street, Fermoy, County Cork.

chapel doorway, etc., etc. The march was carried out and Fermoy grovelled. But – how stupid can the authorities be?! After a few days, when we were top dogs again, they suddenly moved us to – of all places – Cork, from where our assailants had come. We moved into Victoria Barracks (since burnt down) alongside the Ox & Bucks LI. We had a double company detachment about six miles out at Ballincollig. I was with that lot – about half a dozen Subalterns under a Major, who was resigning and emigrating. Except for me, all the Subalterns were ex cavalry war-time promoted 'rankers' (a splendid tough lot). We had to take turns to dine in Mess at Battalion headquarters on 'Guest Nights'. I well remember my turn, as I had to cycle in in Mess Kit and, late at night, as I cycled back in the dark, I rounded a corner between high hedges slap into a parade of 'Sinn Féiners' drilling. They were as much surprised as I was, and they all turned outwards and hung their heads so that I could not see their faces, I don't doubt my hair stood up a bit as I rode silently through! Our Fermoy incident was, I believe, the first incident of bloodshed after the quelling of the '1916 Easter Rising' (looked on by us as a stab-in-the-back, but differently by them!!). Cork was not a happy station. There was soon trouble, started by Sinn Féin gangs cutting off the hair of girls seen to be chatting with soldiers, who naturally resented it. Entrenching-tool handles soon found their real use, up the sleeve, and heads were being cracked and opponents being pushed into the river. So our next move was to the Curragh (County Kildare). But before we go there, I would say that we used to find an 'Officers Guard' on important prisoners in Cork Gaol. I remember more than once being officer of the guard and marching with fixed bayonets from the Barracks the length of Patrick Street and spending my night outside the cell-door of The Countess Marcheviz (I can't spell her!), to be known as the 'Stormy Petrel' of Irish politics. She was of good Irish family (Gore-Booth), but had married a Pole and become a fanatical rebel. I was to meet

The last British Army guard marches out of Dublin Castle, 1921.

her again a half a century later, when I was reluctantly being forced to set foot in Ireland again, to do with some business connected with the death of an aunt of my wife's. I had gone for a stroll in Dublin on St Stephen's Green, which I had known long ago, and found myself alongside a statue. Looking up, it was to see that it was The Countess Marckeviz, as a national heroine!! So our next move – The Curragh, were stationed in Barracks, named after Wellington's famous Peninsular General Beresford, and from appearances, untouched since those days! The Battalion was dispersed with Company Detachments in places like Maryborough and Tullamore, with a smaller detachment at a house on the River Shannon, named Hunston House. Military training was NIL, except for Weapon Training Courses. I had become the Weapon Training Officer and Asst/Adjt. Patrols and raiding parties were often out at nights in pursuit of wanted men required by 'Intelligence'. I recall one particular occasion, when I had been ordered to take my platoon, by night, in a lorry across The Bog of Allan, form a road-block with the idea of capturing a badly wanted 'bad-hat', rumoured likely to come through. Our lorry proved too heavy for the bog road and sank through the surface. At dawn, while we were still endeavouring to get the lorry on to firm ground, a Sergeant of the RIC – that splendid body of men – cycled out from his Police Barrack near Edenderry, to see if he could help. He asked me how I would like his job separated so far from any help. I didn't think I would particularly relish it, but he went on 'of all the ignorant, dirty, cruel and treacherous people commend me to the Irish, and – he went on – I'm an Irishman myself and I have never left Ireland'. I said to him – referring to the crofter-types going off to work – all these chaps seem very polite (touching their caps and saying 'Marnin', Sgt', etc.). He turned to me and disdainfully asked 'Did you ever meet an Irishman who wasn't polite – to your face? You wait until he's gone ten yards past you'!! In view of so much that had happened since (and happens daily) I have never forgotten what he said. In those days the RIC were split up into small isolated police barracks, with their families. One Sinn Féin trick was to ring round and raid and burn. The Army Recruiting notices used to read 'Join the Army and see the World'. It was quite usual to see scrawled under it 'Join the RIC and see the Next World'.

One of the frequent jobs for the soldier was to be sent out at night with a raiding party to try and capture some wanted man. Some of the stories they told about the filth and squalor were very horrible – e.g., whole families in one bed, sleeping alternately head-feet-head and so on. Perhaps nine or ten in the bed, with rows of unempted jerries under the bed. On one occasion the IO saw, in a mirror in the next room, a whole lot of papers being trust down the bosom of a woman. When he suddenly thrust his hand down and pulled them out there was a great to do! Rifles were hidden in peat stacks. We heard stories of arms being moved from A to B in coffins, hearses surrounded by 'mourners'. In County Monaghan we heard of a cache of arms stored under the altar of their church!! Sometimes, when they had gone to great trouble and risk to apprehend some such wanted men (or women), the powers that were would let him (or her) out again as an act of clemency. They continually did that with people like de Valera and so on. Such an attitude got nowhere, and unsettled the Troops. Unluckily our – then – Battalion IO is dead and so is my old friend, who recently died in Kenya, who was Brigade IO. They knew far more than anybody like me could know. Loyalist farmers were continually having their cattle let out and driven miles in the night, often ham-strung and maimed. However, matters generally were not so bad as nowadays in Ulster. One could go to Race Meetings, and visit various studs, like the National Stud at Tullyho or Loder's stud, where the great Pretty Polly was still on view, in foal, as always to Lemberg. We could even go shooting. I was once on a shooting party in Queen's

Company, with the Brigade IO, and several RIC police officers, when we had to withdraw, in fighting formation to our cars, driven off the bog by an armed party of locals! Matters did not always end so peacefully – viz – a tennis party at the home of the Bagot family, when Sinn Féiners opened fire from the surrounding shrubbery and killed a brother of Lord Cornwallis (17th Lancers. He had recently played cricket against us), and brother (also 17th Lancers) of McCreery (12th Lancers) later to become a famous General in North Africa, and also a young RIC officer (Blake). The daughter of the house, a teenage girl seized a horse and rode off across country for help (no good). Her brother was in the Connaught Rangers. Not many years ago I met him here (then an ex-Gloucester) and he told me the full story. It would be tedious to go on. So we transferred to Kilmainham Barracks, in Dublin. On one occasion our Divisional Commander (Jeudwine) driving his wife and daughter to Dublin had been held up by a car-load of Sinn Feiners. They were left stranded, but not before the old lady had gone to war, thrashing right and left with her umbrella. (The daughter later told me the story!) I remember one visitor to the Battalion – A Colonel Montgomery, because he, with some thirteen other officers, was murdered in bed, in the Gresham Hotel, in Dublin on a Sunday morning on what was Bloody Sunday – the real 'Bloody Sunday', not the modern one! A traitor on the staff of the hotel had let the murderers in and shown them the rooms. The hotel was used by officers at Dublin headquarters. They were all shot in bed in the early hours. I was reminded of this by reading *A Field Marshall in the Family* by Brian Montgomery (a Baluchi Colonel brother of 'Monty' where he records their cousin being murdered. I'm glad to say I watched the last wall of that hotel being demolished – later on – when we were in Dublin. The so-called 'Free State' came into being and we (the Army) reverted to the touchline as spectators, while the Free State and Republicans fought it out. I remember dining on the boat at the next table to Michael Collins (who had been so badly wanted!!) on his way to visit Churchill and/or Lloyd-George – a good looking man, with his sinister body guard round him. He was later killed by his own people in their quarrel for power. We had one subaltern (Storey) murdered in the street one night after dining in another Mess. His car was deliberately rammed by another filled with armed men, who just shot and left him lying there. His uncle lived in Merrion Square, which, I gather was excuse enough to shoot him. In this connection I met – only this week at a luncheon party a young ex 'Sapper' officer, whose family home is in Southern Ireland. He had been posted to Ulster; and WO wouldn't change his posting; so he had no alternative but to resign his commission. Otherwise he risked his home being burnt down. Anybody who has visited parts of Eire like County Cork, County Kerry, etc., will know what I mean. Such abominable outrages have always been the accepted custom. – (Just as an example: Castle Hackett in Galway – the home of General Bernard, who was Divisional Commander, 3rd Division in the late 1930s and later our Governor of Bermuda, was burnt down. So was the home of Colonel Head, RA, near Birr, who then bought Hinton in Salop, in the 1920s.) It was to prevent Hunston House being burnt down that we (2nd Battalion) had a Detachment there, refer to above. This detachment suffered a typical Irish ambush. They had a patrol out on bicycles, about half a dozen strong; as they cycled past a stone wall, the ambushers popped up from behind it. The patrol had no alternative but to surrender their rifles. Not a popular incident!! I could quote two other murders of female relatives of two of my former COs, who told me the stories, but perhaps I'd better not!

In Dublin we watched the burning of the Four Courts in the quarrel between Free State and Republicans. We were not participants, but we were told our Gunners had lent the Free Staters a gun to help them; one day I and another (H.P. Miles) were on our way to play cricket at Trinity College, when the traffic was held up and news ran back from 'bus to 'bus that some soldiers had been shot. When we finally reached our 'stop' and were crossing the road, I said to the DM Policeman on point duty, as we passed him, 'is it true that some soldiers have been shot?' He replied 'It is, Sir, three of our men have been shot on the steps of the Post Office'. Foolishly, I said 'Oh, they were Free Staters, were they?' With a blazing face he retorted 'Sir, I said three of our men. I would have you know I was an Irish Guardsman'!! Of course we were in cricket clothes but he knew we were officers. Every Irishman (or girl) was a self-appointed spy. Did I feel 'small'?! But it was a typical incident in that one never knew who was on what side. Another day, a magistrate travelling peaceably on a bus was just shot dead in his seat. The murderers merely walked away, as did those who shot the soldiers. Nobody ever dared to lift a finger. Another time, fire was opened from through the railings alongside Trinity College cricket ground, while a game was in progress against the garrison. A girl, daughter of a Dean, sitting with her fiancé was killed. The assassins just strolled away. The wicket-keeper was Colonel A.F. Spooner, Lancs Fusiliers. He knew he was too heavily equipped to run with any dignity. So he folded his arms and held his ground saying that the British Army would not be driven from the field by a set of gangsters. The other fielders, somewhat shame-facedly reappeared from behind cover and the game continued. Spooner was brother to the famous R.H. (Reggie) Spooner of England fame.

Eventually the 2nd Battalion found the last guard on Dublin Castle and handed over to the relieving guard of the Free State Army (a photo of this is in the Regimental Journal of that time, I think). We didn't suffer from the modern booby-trap and explosive cars, but nobody ever really knew who was who. One day I was on a 'bus filled with troops, on our way back to Kilmainham Barracks, with the Battalion IO. Suddenly I saw him sit up, and opposite to him was a man glaring into his face, with his hand on what was obviously the butt of a revolver in his hip pocket. We were just arriving at the Barrack Gate, and as we got off, I asked him who the man was. He gave me the name of a notorious thug (I think 'Dan Breen') and said 'I arrested him not long ago and he obviously recognised me'. The Free State had come in to being, and he had been let out. Just as well the 'bus was full of troops! It is a sad, sad story and they will (still no doubt) harp on the Battle of the Boyne, because they were defeated there. But read your history! Why was there a battle fought there (1689)? Who was rebelling against whom? Why did England already heavily engaged on the Continent, have to go to the trouble and expense of sending an army there? Ask King Louis XIV of France, and James II, who had been kicked off the English throne and been superceded by 'Orange William' and Mary (James' daughter) – and why?

CHAPTER THIRTEEN

Major Reginald Graham

Details

This is taken from a recording (Accession Number 006181/04) held in the Imperial War Museum's Deparment of Sound Archives. In it Major Graham gives an account on of his time as a boy soldier in the Devonshire Regiment during the War of Independence. He was based in Waterford. He was later commissioned as an officer and spent much of career in the Far East.

Interviewer: Now, one of your early experiences was that you were posted to Ireland during the 'Troubles' there. Can you tell me about your posting there?

RG: Well, we were sent there in July 1920 from Devonport. Headquarters is at Waterford and detachments, companies, were sent out to Wexford, Clonmel, Kilkenny and various other places.

Interviewer: Where did you go?

RG: Waterford.

British Voices

Interviewer: Where were you accommodated there?

RG: In the barracks. There were two barracks in Waterford: the artillery and the infantry barracks. But the infantry barracks was built to accommodate about 200 men but there was about 600 in them till we sent out the detachments. We were sleeping on floors or in tents, barrack room messing etc and so forth.

Interviewer: Was it explained to you what your role was to be there?

RG: Oh, no, no, no, no, you see as a boy I was supposed to be a non-combatant. But I was charged once with whilst on active service leaving my post without being properly relieved. And as the adjutant pointed out to me it carried the death sentence but it didn't worry me. But it happened because the unit had to round up about 200 Sinn Féiners and that called for every man Jack in the Barracks, including the cooks, signallers, they all had to go out and round up these people. And it was decided to put a boy in charge of the telephone exchange. I queried this because I said I knew nothing about telephones, so they said, 'Well, no one will ring through, everyone will be out'. Anyhow, I hadn't sat by myself more than about ten minutes in the cubicle and the flap dropped and a torrent of Morse poured out: dot dot dash dash dash dash. Well, I tried ringing and in the end I left the place to look to see if someone could take down this Morse. Luckily during my absence a signaller from the Royal Corps of Signals who normally manned the wireless station in the barracks heard this tick tick, dot dot dash, went in and took it down. And it was a list of additional men to be rounded up.

Well, Dublin Castle from where the message originated were very annoyed about this and said that someone's head should roll. And the RSM decided that it would be me. Well, I consulted the barrack room lawyer and decided that under the 'old soldiers' act'

208

it wasn't my fault. Anyway, I appeared in front of the adjutant and then in front of the commanding officer and the case was dismissed. And an order was published that in future boys were not to be put on that sort of work.

Interviewer: Did you ever get any impression of the situation in Ireland as far as the 'Troubles' were concerned?

RG: Yes, because we had men wounded, policemen were wounded, ambushes were of a frequent nature, police barracks were attacked and burnt down and there was little or no co-operation between the Royal Irish Constabulary and the troops – at least it seemed to me not to be to the same extent as there is at the present moment in Ulster. They seemed to fade out of it. And then they recruited the Black and Tans who were for all intents and purposes the dirty job boys. You know, they were ex-officers clad in all sorts of uniform, armed with various weapons and they were paid a pound a day. They were really tough people.

Interviewer: Was a pound a day a lot then?

RG: Oh, yes. My pay as a boy was a shilling a day and a full-blown soldier, a fully trained soldier, got four shillings a day.

Interviewer: What did the Army think of the Black and Tans?

RG: We didn't see a lot of them. They'd swoop into barracks, in out, in out, in out. They seemed to have a semi-independent role.

Interviewer: Did you ever see any hostilities yourself in Ireland?

RG: No. I saw the results of them. On January 4th 1921 the police barracks at Tramore was attacked, we sent out a large patrol and luckily the patrol heard a shot go off, the force was split into two and they caught the Shinners crossfire and killed and wounded several. Well, that morning I went into breakfast, at least we were told that breakfast would be in two sittings, and when we went in there was two bodies – naked bodies – laid out on the tables and a man was washing the bodies and plugging up the bullet holes. And as it was rissoles for breakfast that morning not many people ate them.

Interviewer: So these were two soldiers who'd

RG: No, two Shinners. We were very lucky. We had several men wounded but only one fatal one. That was a man that fell into the river at Clonmel on the night patrol clad in battle order.

Interviewer: What was the Army's opinion of the people against whom they were fighting?

RG: Not very much, not very high at all. It was this question of tip and run. You see the ambushes were made chiefly by flying columns. They used to rendezvous at a certain point and the weapons for the ambush were brought out by the women in jaunting cars and things like that. Well, then having counted out the ambush they'd push off and do another one.

Interviewer: Did you take any prisoners of the Sinn Féin?

RG: Oh, yes, yes, yes. But it usually meant at the latter part if they were taken prisoner they were court martialled and shot. For instance in one incident at County Cork four or five men caught digging trenches across the road. They were court martialled at four – if I remember – three or four o'clock on the afternoon and shot

The bodies of two members of the Royal Engineers and two members of the South Staffordshire Regiment in a field near Cork city. They were killed on 10 July 1921.

at half past five. Now the squad that carried out the execution all left Ireland that night because they were on the draft for India. Now it was six men rather and that same night the Shinners went out and picked six British soldiers who were courting girls and shot them. So it was tit for tat.

Interviewer: Did you actually see any prisoners?

RG: Oh, yes, yes, yes, yes, yes. They were brought into the guard room and interrogated by the intelligence officer.

Interviewer: How were they interrogated?

RG: Well, that I don't know but I think under their Marquess of Queensbury Rules, you know, we didn't have any yellow cards or anything to tell us how we should go. For instance if an ambush occurred then the nearest house situated to the ambush was destroyed by the security forces.

Interviewer: What do you mean by yellow card?

RG: Well, what they have in Ireland, in Ulster, at the present moment they have a yellow card which indicates when and how they should open fire. You see over there the challenge was, 'Halt. Hands up. Who are you?'. And if you didn't reply to the challenge then the bloke covering the point of the patrol would open fire. There was an amusing incident once at Kilkenny a patrol was out and a figure loomed up in the darkness and the point of the patrol gave the challenge, 'Halt. Hands up. Who are you?', and the man came rushing forward, he said, 'It's all right soldier I'm Father O'Rourke the parish priest'. And the soldier replied, he said, 'I don't give a bugger if you're Father Christmas', he said, 'you get your bloody hands up'.

Interviewer: And did he?

RG: Oh, yes, quick.

Interviewer: Did anybody actually get shot for not obeying this challenge?

RG: I can only recollect one. Yes, at the same place, Kilkenny. They were taking up the rations under escort of a lance corporal and six men in a limber and the lance corporal heard a scuffle and saw two men trying to wrest the rifle off the rear man of the escort. He shot one of them dead and he saw another man running and said, 'Halt'. The man didn't stop and he shot him dead. And that poor fellow was an ex-serviceman diving for cover.

Interviewer: Were there any consequences for the guard for that?

RG: Oh, no, no, no. There was none of this business of reporting it to the director of public prosecutions.

Interviewer: When you saw the Sinn Féin prisoners what impression of them did you get? Can you describe what they looked like?

RG: Well, they were normally ... I shan't say they were nondescript but they were all, they seemed to be of a certain age group.

Interviewer: What would that be?

RG: About the thirties, early thirties I should say, maybe a bit younger. The older men of course were the commandants as they called themselves, the OCs of the various brigades and whatnot.

The body of Private Fielding of the East Lancashire Regiment lies on a road near Liscarroll, County Cork, 26 April 1921 (above); and (below) after the military ambulance arrived.

Major Reginald Graham

Interviewer: How did they behave under captivity? Quietly or defiantly or what?

RG: Well, there was a lot put in the Kilworth camp, they established an internment camp at Kilworth up in the mountains and dozens of them broke away. Well, I don't think much of an effort was made to recapture them because the treaty was in the offing.

Interviewer: When was this?

RG: 1921 the treaty was signed, the latter part of 1921.

Interviewer: Did you have any dangerous moments yourself in Ireland?

RG: Not myself because I was young, silly, I used to wander miles out into the countryside taking a girl home but nothing was said to me but yet in other cases men had been picked up and shot by (through) associating with Irish girls. You see Cork was the worst place of the lot; they'd be more militant there than anywhere. Cork and Dublin were pretty bad.

Interviewer: So you were courting an Irish girl were you?

RG: Well, you know the usual thing, a lad of fifteen.

Interviewer: Did you feel as you went amongst the population that there was any danger to you?

RG: No, in Waterford ... as a matter of fact the day we left Waterford to come home the local paper printed among other things a tribute to the regiment. They said that during the time

215

they'd been stationed at Waterford the 1st Devons have always upheld the best traditions of the British Army. You see we were not allowed to get out of hand. For instance the Buffs in Fermoy when they heard that the brigadier had been kidnapped they smashed up the town. Matter of fact we used to play the ... the ambush I mentioned previously at Tramore the man that was killed on the bridge had played hockey in Waterford city against the battalion the previous day. So there was a certain amount of ...

Interviewer: Fraternization?

RG: Yes. Slightly but it was there you know.

Interviewer: So the Buffs smashed up Fermoy did they?

RG: Oh, yes. They broke out of camp and smashed up the shops and all that business.

Interviewer: What happened to their brigadier?

RG: Well, he was kidnapped. Brigadier Lucas was fishing on the River Blackwater with his brigade major and, strange as it may seem, they were both released unharmed a week later. One can't imagine that happening today in Ulster.

Interviewer: How did the population at large – the civilian population – behave towards the British troops?

RG: Properly. They were glad we were there because, well, we spent our pay there at the pubs and the what-have-you.

Interviewer: So did you meet any hostility?

RG: Not a lot. They rarely showed it to you, you know, they kept under cover.

Interviewer: How would they show it if they did?

RG: 'English bastard!'

Interviewer: This would be shouted out in the street would it?

RG: Yes, yes, yes.

Interviewer: How did the troops react to that?

RG: Well, 'Irish bastard!'. It was *quid pro quo*.

Interviewer: How did you come to leave Ireland?

RG: Well, when the Treaty was signed all British forces, with the exception of the garrison of Spike Island, were withdrawn.

Interviewer: Were you glad to leave or sorry?

RG: Well, if I say that as we pulled out from the quay at Waterford one soldier said, 'They should have pulled the bloody plug out years ago', because Southern Ireland was poor, there wasn't the industry there that existed in Ulster. It was definitely a poor country.

Interviewer: So what did he mean by 'They should have pulled the plug out'?

RG: Well, let it sink, let Ireland sink into the sea.

Interviewer: So you were glad to leave then were you?

RG: Well, yes, because we were going back to Devonport which was our station – Plymouth – and large garrison town and it was a bit more life, pictures and theatres and what-have-you.

Interviewer: What did the civilian population think of the Black and Tans?

RG: Oh, they loathed them. They hated them.

Interviewer: Why was that?

RG: Well, because the Black and Tans stood absolutely no nonsense. They bashed people about, shot them. And it is suspected that they burnt down the main shopping centre in Victoria Street in Cork after thirteen or fourteen of the chaps had been killed in an ambush.

Interviewer: Do you think that that was true?

RG: Oh, yes, I'm positive.

Interviewer: What makes you so positive?

RG: Well, because it's the sort of thing that they would do there. For instance, they opened up fire at a football match in Dublin once after one of the chaps had been shot – on the crowd.

Interviewer: How did you hear about that?

RG: Well, it was common knowledge in the papers.

Interviewer: How did you know that the civilian population were hostile to the Black and Tans? How did it show itself?

RG: In many ways. You see if a soldier went into a pub he wasn't exactly welcomed with open arms but he was given a drink and they'd talk to him, the publican would, but if the Black and Tans went into a pub there was dead silence.

Interviewer: Would he be served a drink if he asked for one?

RG: Oh, yes. Well, if he wasn't served with a drink he'd jolly well get it.

Interviewer: Get it himself you mean?

RG: Yes. You see they seemed to be a law unto themselves.

CHAPTER FOURTEEN

Major Gerald Stone

Details

This is taken from a recording (Accession Number 006059/03) held in the Imperial War Museum's Dept of Sound Archives. In it Major Stone gives an account on of his service as a junior officer in the Devonshire Regiment during the War of Independence. He was based in Wexford. He later served in Hong Kong and Shanghai in the 1920s.

Interviewer: How did your posting to Ireland come about?

GS: The battalion had gone out there in June 1920, I was at the depot at Exeter at the time, and when I completed my tour of duty at the depot in March '21 I was posted to the battalion. I was a month with the battalion headquarters at Waterford. Then I was posted to Enniscorthy in command of the platoon there having taken over from a real fire-eater who ruled the place with a rod of iron and was unofficially known as the uncrowned king of Enniscorthy.

Interviewer: Who was he known that by?

GS: Well, I think it was by the battalion. One didn't have much contact with many of the outside people, we just had about half a dozen personal friends in Enniscorthy.

Interviewer: Before you went to Ireland did you know very much about the political situation there?

GS: Yes. We knew from what we heard from the battalion, that is, one or two officers at the depot had had letters from officers out there and learnt what it was like and so we gathered from them that was what the situation was?

Interviewer: What did you understand the situation to be?

GS: That you had the IRA, that's who one was up against, and there were ambushes chiefly. There was no gelignite or anything that way. And that's what I understood before going out. After I got out and had experience of it the IRA used to try and prevent our getting along in our Crossley cars which we always moved three cars at a time, 150 yards between each, so that if any were ambushed only one, at the outside two, would be in the ambush. And you had them blocking the roads in three different ways. One, they would cut a trench nearly across the road just leaving room for a jaunty car to go round – that's the little Irish horse-drawn vehicle. To compete with that we used to carry planks so that we'd put these down across the trench, then they'd cut trees down across the road and they were too difficult to deal with and you would look for a gate one side of the tree leading to a field and then a gate the far side to see if you could get round the tree that way. If you couldn't then you would probably have to take another road.

And the third way they used to try and ... this was to destroy the back axle of the Crossley to break it ... they used to put potholes for

A combined patrol of the British Army and RIC in action during an ambush in County Clare.

about 100 yards all down the road so the Crossley coming along at speed would go bump, bump, bump, and the back axle which was a weak part of those Crossleys would possibly break.

Another nasty thing they used to do, about dusk they would put a piece of wire, or barbed wire, across the road neck high to catch people sitting in front in the neck there. And that being the case if when we had an armoured Crossley we used to put that in front to break the wire that night so that nobody was injured.

A friend of mine I knew could only speak like this [whispers] ... for the rest of their life because they were caught in the wire.

Interviewer: Was he the only casualty you knew of that kind?

GS: There were casualties in ambushes and one always had – when the road was blocked – to see that there was no ambush. [That was] the first thing one did before dealing with crossing the trench or getting round the tree. I wasn't quite sure what your ...

Interviewer: I meant that did you ...

GS: That was the only one I heard had been caught in the net, yes. I wasn't sure whether you meant that.

Interviewer: That's what I meant.

GS: Yes.

Interviewer: Did you know of any Crossley tenders which had had their back axles broken by their methods?

GS: No, I didn't, and none in the battalion did and I didn't hear of any outsiders – being only a subaltern I probably wouldn't.

Interviewer: Did you actually experience any ambushes yourself?

GS: No, I didn't, no. If we went out we'd go out one way and come back another road so that they wouldn't be lying up for us on the road we'd gone out by.

Interviewer: Did you go on a large number of patrols?

GS: Quite a few. Usually when one of the police barracks in my area were shot up – or had just a few shots fired at it which was a trick of the IRA to get the Army out and ambush them on the way out. But I never had any experience of ambushes. But if you'd like me to go on about a friend of mine?

Interviewer: Yes, please.

GS: He was stationed at Waterford and the Tramore Police Barracks had shots fired at it, and he was in mufti but the subaltern in charge of the party to go out was just new from Sandhurst and so he thought he'd better go with the party. And so off they went and they were ambushed on the way and it was the young subaltern's Crossley that was ambushed.

But this officer in mufti found out where the firing was coming from. It was coming from a hedge overlooking the road. His vehicle wasn't ambushed. And he went along that hedge – using his revolver as a humane killer – and killed about a dozen of them. They were so busy firing on to the road they didn't realise what was happening.

And the IRA put up a memorial to the twelve who were killed in the Tramore ambush at the spot where the ambush took place. And this happened in 1921 and a private soldier in the battalion went across to Waterford in 1939 – that is eighteen years later – and in a pub he just mentioned that he was out there with the Devons in 1921 and a chap from the far end of the bar came along, 'You were in the Devons were you?' and produced a photo of this particular officer who was in mufti, and, 'Well, do you know this officer?'. And so the chap, 'Oh, no, I don't know him' – of course he did really. And he said, 'Well, if you see him tell him we're still after him'.

That officer was ordered by the colonel to leave Ireland next day and he was seconded to West Africa because he said to this officer, 'Your life will not be worth a minute's purchase if you remain here any longer. They'll get you'.

Interviewer: Can you remember what his name was?

GS: As he's dead now I will. His name was Valentine.

Interviewer: What was the morale like of your unit in Ireland?

GS: It was very high. We knew we were getting the better of the IRA. In my platoon detachment there were no trees cut down for trenches or any sign of activity within three miles of Enniscorthy itself.

Interviewer: Was Enniscorthy a village or a town?

GS: It was a little market town. And those on the run used to come in for, I suppose, a bath, a change of clothes, and we used to go out to visit places that we knew these chaps were, their home was, about twice a week. And it was always the old mother who used to answer the door and the look of relief on her face when she saw it was us and not the IRA because she was so frightened that the IRA had come along to take off the next son who was coming up to manhood. And I suppose it wouldn't have been if the chap had been in the house. Now I could tell a story about that type of thing if you'd like to hear.

Interviewer: Please.

GS: Just before war broke out I was garrison adjutant, Devizes, and the first night I was there I was called to the telephone and there was obviously a Southern Irishman (as) the telephone orderly. And after I'd finished the call I said to him 'You're from Southern Ireland aren't you?'. 'Yes, sir'. 'What's your name?'. 'O'Connor, sir', then I asked him where he came from, he said, 'Enniscorthy, sir'. I said, 'Any relation to Ginger O'Connor?'. A look of surprise in his face. 'That's my brother, sir'. I said, 'Well, I'm going to put you in the picture. We were after your brother, he was on the run and one night we nearly got him, his bed was warm.' I always used to send the first party round the back of the house, the second party in front and the third party I used to go in and Ginger O'Connor had just got over the wall at the back before my chaps got there. The telephone orderly said, 'Well, sir, you hadn't got much chance really as I was a small boy of eight and we small boys were posted round Enniscorthy and any movement of you from the courthouse' – which was our billets – 'noise was spread abroad that you were out and everybody on the run skedaddled straight away'.

Interviewer: How did the Army treat the civilians in these searches?

GS: On the whole very well. There was an instance where a watch was stolen. When the woman came out saying her watch was stolen I immediately ordered the chaps to put their hats on the ground, turn out their pockets, keeping their pockets open and put everything in their hats, and there was no sign of the watch. But in a pawnbrokers later the watch appeared and the name of the chap appeared and we got him for theft on that evidence.

Interviewer: So he was one of your unit, was he?

GS: He was, yes. But that was the only trouble I had with them.

Interviewer: Was he punished for the theft?

GS: Yes, definitely.

Interviewer: What punishment did he get?

GS: Oh, I've forgotten these days – my memory's not like it was – in my old age.

Interviewer: Did the Army do any damage in these searches?

GS: No, we were very careful not to. And in these houses we found hens in wardrobes nesting and we always picked up fleas. And I used to average about three fleas after each search that we took. That's after the truce, the late summer of 1921, instead of having a rat week I had a flea week where we all, and the dogs, got Keatinged and scrubbed and ...

Interviewer: The dogs got what?

GS: Scrubbed and Keating's Powder, you know, for fleas.

Interviewer: Did you have any Black and Tan Unit in your area?

GS: Yes. We were on a round-up exercise, we knew that the IRA were on the mountains, and we formed a block in one particular village. And the Black and Tans came along to the village when I was out on patrol and they nearly shot my sentry. The Black and Tans were a darned nuisance, they were a lot of ex-officers out of a job after the First War, and where we tried to make friends with the local Irish they just antagonised them completely.

Interviewer: How did they do that?

GS: By their behaviour in ... I was going to say in everyway, in any way you can think of.

Interviewer: Can you give me an example?

GS: In their dealings with the locals they treated them rough. I believe they used to have a lot of drunks and rather on that line. I've no experience of that of course, I was just told that.

Interviewer: What did the Army think of the Black and Tans?

GS: Oh, we didn't like them. They were dealing with the IRA the way the IRA should be dealt with but it was with the civilian population that we didn't like them, their behaviour towards them.

Interviewer: What were the relations like between the Army and the civilian population?

GS: Very good. As best as one could expect.

Interviewer: How did this show itself?

GS: Well, oh, I think any way that friendly relations could be. That is, we went to dances, we played hockey with civilians and they were quite pleased to see us. There was no trouble with the troops and civilians. I had no complaints from the police or civilians about the troops' behaviour.

Interviewer: Did you ever meet with any hostility from the civilians?

GS: Not actual. When we joined the hockey club we were told that the local chemist and one of the doctors at the lunatic asylum which was outside, they refused to play hockey as long as we played. And so I said to the chap running the hockey, 'Look, would you rather we didn't play?', and, 'Oh, no, we want you to play. If they don't want to play that's up to them'. I said, 'Well, don't you consider that we should not play because we'll be leaving and what will happen after we leave?'. 'Oh, no, don't let that worry you. We want you to play'.

Interviewer: You were talking earlier about knowing the name of this Ginger O'Connor who was on the run. How did you get such intelligence?

GS: I think it was … We got it from the Royal Irish Constabulary as they were in those days.

Interviewer: And what opinion did you have of the Royal Irish Constabulary as a force?

GS: Oh, mainly a very high opinion. They were excellent at their job, those I dealt with, and I couldn't speak higher – the Royal Irish Constabulary.

Interviewer: Now you mentioned the patrols that you were on and the occasional attacks of the IRA on barracks. Did you see any other action in Ireland?

GS: No

CHAPTER FIFTEEN

Major General Hawes

Details

This is taken from an unpublished autobiography held in the Department of Documents at the Imperial War Museum. Major General Hawes began his career at the Royal Military Academy at Woolwich and from there joined the Royal Garrison Artillery. He served as a staff officer in World War One, serving in France, Italy and in the occupation of Germany. After the war, he served in Ireland from 1919 to 1920, and in India for two tours, 1920 to 1923 and 1932 and 1937. In the inter-war years, he also served at the War Office and with the General Staff. During the Second World War, he served in the Home Forces, and was Commander of the South Midland District from 1942 to 1945. After the War, he became Controller of the Home Department BRCS, a position which he held until 1957.

SERVING WITH ME at general headquarters and living in our mess, was Major Gordan Primsdale RE. When I went on leave in January 1919, I stayed the weekend with his family. There I first met Molly, my future wife. In May 1919 I was at home again and this time went

The Grand Parade, Cork, c. 1900.

to a dance with her. We became engaged at this dance. We were married at her home in Uxbridge on October 4th 1919.

There began then more than 50 years of married life. For my part I had found a partner who for more than 50 years became my strength and my stay, always at hand to encourage and to defend, steadfast in our successes and courageous in disasters.

I cannot say more, except that the description of what a perfect wife should be, given in the Bible, might have been written about her.

Now she has left me, with a void that nothing will ever fill. It was always my prayer that she should go first and that she should not suffer a long illness – both these prayers were granted.

I firmly believe that our dear ones are near us in point of space and very close in point of time, and that Molly and our son, Grahame, who died in Norway in 1939, are waiting for me. This is my hope and my consolation.

We had one night at the Berkeley Hotel and one night at Uxbridge, by way of a honeymoon and then crossed to Cork where I was to become Staff Captain of the Cork District. My orders were to join immediately. When I reported for duty, I found there was literally nothing to do. We had fourteen battalions of the four Irish regiments and their regimental depots.

There were no men in these battalions and we were not allowed to employ the depot personnel outside barracks. The reason for this was that Sinn Féin activity was growing and it was felt undesirable to ask our men to engage their brothers.

My only work was each Saturday morning to sign a return showing how many rats had been killed during the week. This is a fact. To add to my frustration with my work, I had come from a very active and essential appointment to a useless one. I had also come down in rank, and very much down in pay, from a Major to a captain.

The great access of leisure time was for a little most welcome.

The Changing of the Guard; the British Army departs Richmond Barracks as the new National Army enters, 1922.

We used to play golf at a course about five miles out of Cork. Then the troubles got worse and our movements became more and more restricted, until we were virtually confined to barracks.

I tried to transfer to the local infantry brigade and was promised an appointment, but my Brigadier refused to let me go, I think because this would expose the futility of his and my appointment.

The soldiers despised the Sinn Féiners. They never came into the open. All the shooting was in the back from behind walls. When cornered as in a search for arms on a bridge, the ends of which had been closed, the men handed their revolvers to the women, who hid them under their skirts. Men were searched but women never. The priests played an active part and would extol, as feat of arms, the murder of an unarmed policemen pulled off a bus, and shot by a gang of thugs and left lying in the road.

More and more troops were poured into Southern Ireland until there were some 100,000 of them. Techniques for quelling the rebellion were perfected and the rebellion was being subdued. HM Government chose this moment to give in. All the casualties we had suffered were wasted. While it might have been wise to give Southern Ireland independence, I feel this might well have been done much earlier or kept until we had made it quite clear that we were acting from a position of strength.

The murder of a number of officers in their beds in Dublin was a great shock to the army. It was hailed by the Sinn Féiners as a major victory.

I had no contact with the 'Black and Tans'. These men had all had active service, many of them with very distinguished records. All were tough. They met the rebels on level terms and beat them at their own game. This was the reason for their extreme unpopularity.

The regular soldier, as always, was fair game. He had to wait to be shot at before he could retaliate. Any action of his which caused damage to the rebels was raised in the newspapers and often in

British gunners and artillery on board a ship during the evacuation from Dublin, 1922.

Parliament. In short, military service in Ireland at that time was wholly and heartily disliked.

At the moment of writing this, British Troops in Ulster are receiving the same treatment and the same ingratitude. General Freeland's remark on television about the troops leaving Ulster, made a few days ago were, I am sure, said against a background of the supreme test of discipline they were experiencing.

A small example of the mentality of the Southern Irishman came my way when I landed at Waterford for the first time. I was waiting in a hotel for my train. With me was a relatively well-educated man. Not knowing how delicate were religion and politics as a subject of conversation, I allowed myself to be engaged in a discussion of them. Suddenly he pointed at a tower, obviously of great age, and said 'When King John came here to receive the allegiance of the Irish Kings, he made them kiss his foot and laughed at their clothes. This,' he said, 'was an example of the behaviour of the hated English'. He went on from there to Cromwell.

In October 1920, Molly became ill with terrible headaches and vomiting. She was on the point of going home on leave. I was to follow in a few days. By the grace of God she got home safely, but three days later went down with typhoid fever. The water supply in Cork was contaminated. She was at the point of death for days on end. She lost two or three stone in weight and when I got home I found a skeleton.

At this time we were confined to barracks, having been informed that all officers out alone were liable to be shot. I was closing my official accounts and organising my cash for leave. I could not go down to the bank in the city, so took £50 of public money from the safe and put in a cheque of my own.

Two days later the bank rang up to say it had been dishonoured. I sent a telegram to Molly's father and he transmitted the necessary money to Cork. I went and redeemed my cheque. When I

Members of the new National Army on parade in Dublin, 1922.

went to Cox-Kings in London to complain, they laughed. I could have got damages I was told but didn't press the matter because I gathered that the offending clerk would be severely punished.

When I left Cork, I went down alone to the quay. When I went to get my ticket, two men with black hombourg hats and hands in coat pockets came up, one either side of me. They read my name on my warrant over my shoulder. I watched them in the glass of the booking clerks window. I was not wanted I suppose and so was allowed to embark. I was not happy till we got to sea. The reason I was not molested on the quay might have been, I heard later, because a Sinn Féiner on the run was escaping on the same ship.

FURTHER READING

Aggett, W.J.P., *The Bloody Eleventh: History of the Devonshire Regiment*, Vol. III 1915 to 1969, The Devonshire and Dorset Regiment, Wyvern Barracks, Exeter, 1995

Atkinson, C.T. *The South Wales Borderers, 24th Foot, 1689-1937*, Cambridge University Press, Cambridge, 1937

Cowper, Col. J.M., *The King's Own: The Story of a Royal Regiment*, *Vol. III 1914 to 1950*, Gale & Ploden Ltd, Aldershot, 1957

Crozier, Brig. General F.P., *Impressions and Recollections*, Werner Laurie, London, 1930

Gurney, Lt. Col. Russell, *History of the Northamptonshire Regiment, 1742-1934*, Gale & Ploden Ltd, Aldershot, 1935

Macready, General Sir Nevil, *Annals of An Active Life, George H. Doran*, New York, 1925

Powell, Geoffrey, *The History of the Green Howards: Three Hundred Years of Service, Arms and Armour*, London, 1992

Wylly, Col. H.C., *History of the Manchester Regiment, Vol I, 1883 – 1925*, Forester Groom, London, 1925.

INDEX

Other Titles from The Collins Press

The IRA in Kerry 1916-1921

Sinead Joy

The traditional view of the IRA in Ireland from 1916-1921 – of heroes only living for the republic – has come in for close scrutiny in recent years. This study dispels some of the myths and gives an alternative profile of the rebels active in Kerry. It questions their reasons for joining and their commitment to the notion of the republic. The result is sometimes critical as it considers the effects of the war on Kerry's civilian population and the varying level of support for the IRA. Overall this book presents an account of the perceptions of the community as a awhole, Irish or British, Catholic or Protestant, fighter or civilian.

ISBN: 1-903464-79-X • Price €15.00 PB • 2005

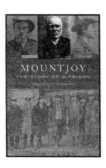

Mountjoy: The Story of a Prison

Tim Carey

Open a window on Mountjoy's remarkable history. It is an epic story with a cast of over half a million, from staff to vicious murderers and famous figures in Irish history. This story is intertwined with historical issues and events that set it in a broader context.

ISBN: 1-903464-89-6 • Price €14.95 PB • 2004

Over the Bar:
A Personal Relationship with the GAA

Breandán O hEithir

Growing up on the Aran Islands Breandán O hEithir became a passionate follower of hurling and football. After dropping out of university, a variety of jobs brought him into close contact with the GAA all over Ireland. He developed a deep interest in its social life and folklore plus the warmth and fun behind the official goings-on. Here he records his memories of journeys to matches, great players and personalities, and pays tribute to the dynamic and enduring influence of this organisation on Irish society.

ISBN: 1-903464-74-9 • Price € 12.95 PB • 2005

Serving a City
The Story of Cork's English Market

Diarmuid Ó Drisceoil and Donal Ó Drisceoil

This is the first history of Ireland's most famous food emporium, Cork's English Market. Many people have passed through its gates since its establishment in 1788. Though the products on sale now may be more cosmopolitan, the energy and essence of the market remain the same. This book traces the history and development of the market from its origins to the present day, with historic and recent photographs, architectural plans, reproductions of paintings and other illustrations.

ISBN: 1-903464-72-2 • Price € 27.95 HB • 2005

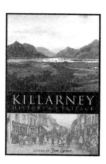

Killarney – History and Heritage

Editor: Dr Jim Larner

Killarney forms the backdrop for most visits to Kerry. Since its foundation in 1754 it has attracted more visitors than any part of Ireland and inspired generations of poets and painters. To mark the 250th anniversary of the founding of Killarney town, this comprehensive collection of essays was compiled. It describes Killarney's history and heritage from prehistoric to modern times, including folklore, sporting history, architecture and film. This lavishly illustrated book is an enjoyable, informative read for the general and more serious reader alike.

ISBN: 1-903464-55-2 • Price €24.95.00 HB • 2005

The Irish Draught Horse – A History

Mary McGrath and Joan C. Griffith

The Irish draught horse is an icon in the Irish landscape. Through good times and bad it was a constant companion, the work horse which pulled the farmers' plough, took the family to church, hunted, was a draught animal and pulled field artillery. Today the Irish draught is used for hunting, for pleasure and competition, much valued by a new generation of owners. Here the story of the 'horse of the people' is told before facts and details vanish forever.

ISBN: 1-903464-82-X • Price €25.00 HB • 2005

Stone Upon Stone
The Use of Stone in Irish Building
Nicholas Ryan

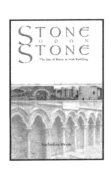

Stone has been used for building in Ireland for over 6,000 years. The earliest farmers arrived about 4000 BC and found stone was a valuable building material. Since then, stone has left imprints in Irish history, culture and folklore, as it was a natural resource available throughout the whole island. While many books deal with related subjects, such as national monuments, bridges and castles, this subject has never before been examined in chronological sequence.

ISBN: 1-903464-91-9 • Price €15.00 PB • 2005

Croke Park
A History
Tim Carey

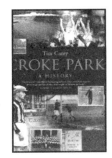

Headquarters of our largest sporting and cultural organisation, the GAA, its arena has witnessed many dramas. Thousands have played on its stage while millions have watched. Today it is one of the world's most impressive stadiums – the third largest in Europe – and a symbol of the GAA's strength. This history tells the story of 'Croker'.

ISBN: 1-903464-54-4 • Price €30.00 HB • 2004

A Doctor's War
Aidan MacCarthy
INTRODUCTION BY PETE MCCARTHY

Researching *McCarthy's Bar* Pete McCarthy entered MacCarthy's Bar in Castletownbere, west Cork. While there Adrienne MacCarthy gave him a copy of her father's wartime memoir. Pete found it 'unputdownable'. An RAF medical officer, Aidan served in France, survived Dunkirk, and was plunged into adventures in the Far East. In Nagasaki his life was literally saved by the dropping of the atomic bomb and he was an eyewitness to the horror and devastation it caused.

ISBN: 1-903464-70-6 • Price ¤12.95 PB • 2005

As Others Saw Us
Cork Through European Eyes
Editors: Joachim Fischer and Grace Neville
This anthology contains views and opinions by continental writers about Cork from medieval times to the present. The varied texts include excerpts from travel books, essays, newspaper articles and memoirs. Each piece has a brief introduction about its author and the context in which it was written. The foreign langauge is on one page and the English translation opposite. Designed to appeal to the general rather than specialist reader, the excerpts are short and from the widest variety of viewpoints.

ISBN: 1-903464-85-4 • Price ¤18.95 PB • 2005